An Introduction To Spiritualism

An Introduction To Spiritualism

S. Jeffery & D. Underdown

Illustrations by S. Bolton

AMHERST

ISBN 1 903637 40 6

Printed in Great Britain

First published in 2006 by

Amherst Publishing Limited
Longmore House, High Street, Otford, Sevenoaks, Kent TN14 5PQ

This book is dedicated to our mothers, for without their love and support over the years we would not be the people we are today. Our thanks to you both with lots of love. Also special thanks to Bill for his support and belief in us. S. & D.

Authors' Erratum to 'An Introduction to Spiritualism'

As authors it is imperative that our book is honest and factually accurate. Unfortunately, despite efforts to the contrary, we too have fallen victim to the many fallacies that plague Spiritualism due to its diversity of belief and the under-publicised historical data held within the Spiritualist Movement as a whole. We apologise for any misguidance and it is our intention to correct this through the following amendments:

Pg 25 states "...Spiritualism gained recognition from the Government in 1954. As such Spiritualism became one of only two officially recognised religions in the UK." No primary legislation has been passed to this effect. However, it is believed that this statement's origins lie in King Henry VIII's introduction of the Statute of Proclamations, 1539 which gave him power to legislate by proclamation. To this end it is contested by some that in 1954 such a proclamation was passed elevating Spiritualism to the same status as other religions and as such became only one of two to be recognised in the UK in this way. Our research to conclusively verify the above continues.

Pg 74 William Tyndale (c.1492-1536). Our critics question Tyndale's inclusion stating that he was not a Spiritualist. We agree; he was not. His inclusion merely served to highlight the injustice of the followers of Christianity of the day and at no time do we state that he was a Spiritualist.

Pg 86 & 104 Spiritualist National Union. This should read Spiritualists' National Union

Pg 116 "This report was leaked to the media in 1979..." This should read "This report was officially released in 1979..."

Pg 213 www.members.tripod.com This website has now moved to www.helenduncan.org.uk

PREFACE

In the planning of this book, it was always our intention to provide an interesting, informative and educational guide to Spiritualism. As is clearly suggested in the title, our initial and primary focus was upon the production of an honest and plain-speaking introduction to Spiritualism aimed at what we humbly consider to be a misinformed and unaware public. We say 'initial' because during our extensive research we became increasingly aware of the gaps in the knowledge of even those previously initiated into the Spiritualist beliefs. It soon became apparent that it was the sheer diversity within these beliefs that created an immense accumulation of knowledge which was too vast to absorb over a short period of time. It also became increasingly clear that any attempt to produce a definitive guide to Spiritualism would be too enormous and time consuming as a project.

Although as stated our primary focus was to promote public awareness towards Spiritualism, the book also gave us an opportunity to realise a secondary aim; the introduction to our own organisation; ETVOS. This is an acronym for Enlightenment; The Voice Of Spirit and was created with the guidance of Spirit in order to raise the awareness of Spiritualism through education, philosophy, training and research. We are autonomous and as such are neither associated with, connected nor affiliated to, any other organisation, church, centre or group. Our organisation is based upon four simple Principles which go some way in showing that, unlike some organisations within the Spiritualist Movement, we choose not to adopt a Christian-based status:

1. Continuation of life after the death of the physical body for all.
2. Taking responsibility for your actions.
3. Respect for all individuals.
4. One God fits all.

Within the book we take the opportunity to reveal our basic tenets and philosophy, just as we do those of our main Spiritualist counterparts, to allow everyone to see for themselves the diversity within our Movement. Also we attempt to alleviate the fear factor through the bringing of a greater understanding of Spiritualist beliefs and how we exercise them. In doing so, we hopefully clear up numerous myths and misconceptions currently held by the general public. We never consciously set out to single out any of the orthodox faiths that have in the past and in many cases still do, attack or condemn Spiritualism. However, that said, we make no apologies for upsetting the anti-Spiritualists during our attempts to 'put the record straight', for we are certainly not afraid of controversy and have no intention of shying away from it when it can instigate healthy debate that can serve to put a stop to spiritual deprivation.

So whatever your religious belief, if any, and whatever the reason is for you to have chosen to read this book, we can only hope that you do so with an open mind, an unbiased reasoning and that you find at least some of the contents thought provoking. Enjoy.

CONTENTS

An Introduction to Spiritualism
By S Jeffery & D Underdown

Authors Erratum

As from the 26th May 2008 the Fraudulent
Mediums Act 1951 c.3 was repealed and
replaced by the Consumers Protection
from Unfair Trading Regulations 2008
(1277).

FOREWORD

Spiritualism is the leper of the religious world. Our greatest challenge comes from the Christian-based faiths, for they believe that as Spiritualists we consort with the Devil and are therefore a danger to society. This unfounded misconception is entrenched in centuries of literalist and fundamentalist interpretations of the Bible.

At times it may seem that we are being harsh towards Modern day religions, particularly the Christian-based faiths, but all we are trying to do is show the hypocrisy and injustice meted out against Spiritualists by emphasising our points of view. No religion is perfect including Spiritualism. All faiths have their flaws, as well as good and bad points. As Spiritualists, all we want is world recognition as enjoyed by Christianity, Islam, etc. Our spiritual stance on life is as valid as any other religion, and yet we are constantly being slated for our beliefs. Why? If it were aimed at any other popular religion there would, without doubt, be a public outcry, and yet our outcries are not considered valid or are withheld from public attention.

As Spiritualists, we believe that all roads lead to God irrespective of your beliefs; atheist, agnostic, Christian, Muslim, Jewish, Buddhist, Spiritualist, whatever. What is important is not so much the belief system, if any, but the individual - you, and how you live your life. There is no Devil and definitely no single religion that has the right to a monopoly on God, for ONE GOD FITS ALL.

We have experienced people recoiling in horror, running away from us, as well as the elitist bigotry of religions and all in response to what they believe we represent. As Spiritualists you could say we are partly responsible for the negative attitude towards us because, as a movement, we do not publicly defend our beliefs. Then again, with such opposition it has proven to be a difficult task, especially considering that we don't have the financial 'clout' of the older, more established religions.

Confusion in understanding who we are and what we represent can also be attributed to the wide variety of informational mediums associated with Spiritualism at this present time. These include the so-called 'Mind, Body and Spirit' books with numerous authors relating their personal perspectives upon such topics as psychic development, Angels, crystals, and witchcraft, to name but a few. Then there are the ever increasing number of TV shows with 'Spiritualistic' Mediums from both the UK and USA, either offering 'readings' in a studio or visiting places that have reportedly had Spirit activity of some sort or another. Finally there are the increasingly popular newspaper and magazine advertisements for postal or telephone Psychic and tarot readings, not to mention the all-new psychic dating and compatibility offers.

All these elements contribute to the giving of a very confusing message with regards to Spiritualism in general. Spiritualism is not about divination, however, it has absorbed the use of divination tools such as crystals, runes and tarot cards, to such an extent that there is public confusion, particularly with terminology that is interchangeable. The public image does not differentiate between Psychic and Spiritualist Mediums. However, there is a very distinct difference and one that should be recognised by the general public, especially when paying for their services.

Despite a recent upsurge in exposure there is in fact a limited amount of valuable philosophical information available to the general public concerning Spiritualism. When was the last time you watched a popular religious programme where a representative of Spiritualism - not a Psychic - was invited to join a religious debate? Never, to our knowledge. It is in everybody's interest to be able to read and learn about the many facets of Spiritualism, but to date, we have not come across what can be described as a definitive guide to Spiritualism in the high street bookshops. There are of course books attributed to psychic development as there are those concerning linking with Spirit Guides/Angels, but what we are somewhat lacking is material that differentiates between the two and this to us is of great importance indeed.

With regards to the TV exposure; although it is good to be able to view Spiritualist Mediums demonstrating their abilities in front of a studio audience, we would like to see more time allocated to the philosophical side of Spiritualism. Maybe this is down to the limitation of time or the network's lack of desire to show this as it is not what they consider entertainment. Either way, Spiritualism is the loser. We would also like the leading bodies of our Movement to create more exposure 'for the cause' so to speak, despite the fact that whenever the opportunity arises their words are manipulated or edited to the satisfaction and/or ideals of those in the production/direction seats. Never forget; there is no such thing as impartial reporting!

Why is it that TV generally stereotypes Mediums as being eccentric, weird, middle-aged and with a questionable IQ? The answer is: To boost ratings and offer a cheap form of entertainment, while playing down our respectability as a religion.

So what is the best means for a member of the general public to find out more about Spiritualism? The internet is a good source, although it does give negative, positive, even eccentric views of the Movement, so we advise the use of reason/common sense. The other source of information is through actual attendance of a Spiritualist church/centre, but it is not always easy to locate such a place. Growth in numbers is often attributed to word of mouth rather than good advertising as outlets for this are limited. From personal experience we have found that once people realise we are Spiritualists they withdraw their consent to allow the holding of our religious services/public demonstrations in their buildings. Often costs can be inexplicably elevated as a deterrent to any form of long term access and some so-called spiritual religions can be so elitist in their attitude as to blatantly abuse your beliefs in response to an inquiry over location sharing. Advertising can be an expensive exercise even when the cause is a charitable one, especially if required on a regular basis.

However, once people find their local Spiritualist establishment they may attend through curiosity or because they seek comfort and reassurance through a time of personal grief. Others would like to attend but don't, through a combination of fear of what they might hear or see and that they may be pressurised to attend on a regular basis against their will. Some fear ridicule from friends and/or family based on common misconceptions of Spiritualists and their services. A few will stay away preferring to use other attendees for feedback.

The truth is that the role played in society by their local Spiritualist church/centre is one of providing a forum where philosophy is taught and proof of survival (the afterlife) is given. Mediums serve to link attendees with the Spirit World and where possible to offer guidance to those seeking their spiritual pathway or answers to make sense of their life, or even life in general. Once that person has learnt what they needed, they have the freedom of choice to either move on or stay. Unlike many of the orthodox religions, the aim is not to convert but to allow the individual to express freewill in choosing their faith/spiritual pathway without pressure or hindrance.

We, as Spiritualists, are not bad people to be avoided at all costs just because our beliefs and philosophy on life and death are considered fundamentally different from those of the mainstream religions. We believe in an afterlife, but the difference in beliefs begins with the fact that we believe in communication with those that have passed through 'death' into the afterlife. We are merely a bridge as they fulfil their desire to communicate with us offering words of reassurance, encouragement and love, but more than that they offer proof of life beyond physical existence. They feel the need to reassure us that they are safe and well, still looking out for us, guiding us and comforting us through our time of grief.

This guidebook is not definitive because Spiritualism is so diverse a subject, but hopefully will bring a better understanding of Spiritualist beliefs into the public domain, to clarify the difference between Psychic and Spiritualist Mediums, and help replace the fear with a respect for another person's religious/ personal beliefs and a fundamental right to practice them.

The introduction of the Human Rights Act went some way in gaining freedom of practice and a more equal opportunity to appear in the different mediums such as TV, without the fear of censorship.

Human Rights Act 1998

Article 9 - Freedom of thought, conscience and religion:

> 1. Everyone has the right to freedom of thought, conscience and religion; this right includes freedom to change his religion or belief and freedom, either alone or in community with others and in public or private, to manifest his religion or belief, in worship, teaching, practice and observance.

WHAT
IS
SPIRITUALISM?

"Was it something I said?"

SPIRITUALISM

Spiritualism is based upon psychic phenomena and two basic tenets:

- Continuation of life beyond the 'death' of the physical body.
- Communion with Spirit.

Spiritualism is a combination of the ethical approach to life of the Greek philosophers, where you take responsibility for your actions, and the religious concern for the individual's destiny after 'death'- the continued existence of the lifeforce, albeit in a different form; the religious after-life aspect. As with the Greek philosophers, Spiritualists are concerned with this reality and how we live and interact with other people. From the Spirit World we draw strength, faith and guidance, in the knowledge that both sides of the 'veil' are working on behalf of God.

It is important at this early stage, that we take the opportunity to draw your attention to what we consider an important issue of terminology: Whenever reference is made to the term 'lifeforce', as we have in both the first point and paragraph above, it also serves to represent the terms 'soul' and 'spirit' as well. Unless used in quotes or in reference to other organisations, etc., we use it merely because it is our preferred term.

Spiritualism and divination

Many people within the Spiritualist Movement are drawn to crystals, runes, tarot, etc., that are based in ancient divinations. It is here we wish to clarify that Spiritualism in its true form, is not about divination, it is about communing with Spirit; mind to mind between Medium and Spirit. The misconception is that the Spiritualist Medium can prophesise; predict your future. In reality, Spirit can only offer advice and guidance concerning events in your life, but it is up to you the individual to decide whether or not to heed that advice.

For a Spiritualist Medium to offer predictions for your future would suggest that the future is pre-set, 'set in stone' as it were. This cannot be true, for it would remove the most vital ingredient of your spiritual being; freewill. It is this freewill to choose what you do and where you go that constantly alters the future as a whole and not just that of the individual. A word of caution: Spirit may mete out advice that you consider 'bad', but they do so because they perceive the spiritual rewards from the lesson to be learnt of a greater value than a short term 'fix'.

The use of divination tools within Spiritualism plays an important role insomuch as they are used as tools to help the novice develop their psychic abilities, that ultimately if developed further, will create a telepathic link with the Spirit World. There are many Spiritualist Mediums/Psychics who use these methods very successfully to give readings. However, the reality is that if they can link with Spirit then they do not need these aesthetics tools, even though they may enjoy using any particular one. It is the aesthetic values; the beauty and artistry of the tools, that creates the attraction that in turn leads to public demand and goes someway to creating the illusion that a message can be more readily accepted through this format than accepting the fact it is from a separate 'dead' intelligence.

Spiritualism: Religion or cult?
An unpublicised, little known fact, is that following the repeal of the Witchcraft Act and the subsequent introduction of the Fraudulent Mediums Act in 1951, Spiritualism gained recognition from the Government in 1954. As such Spiritualism became one of only two officially recognised religions in the UK. Incidentally, the other recognised religion is the Church of England, and its recognition only came about in order to establish a means of

securing a divorce for Henry VIII from his Catholic wife, Catherine of Aragon.

The irony is that the Christian-based religions consider Spiritualism to be a cult and yet we could say that the majority of the Christian faiths, practicing in the UK, are in effect cults themselves, as it is they who are not on the Statute books of England and Wales, unlike Spiritualism. Consider this; a cult leader requires total devotion from his followers, as well as a monetary input. How many Christian-based religions can you name that encompass these criteria?

Religious trends

In December 2004, the Telegraph newspaper's religious correspondent Jonathan Petre, reported that there were over 170 different faiths or belief systems in Britain. He revealed the statistics collated in a 2001 census of religious affiliation, which placed Spiritualism in 8th place in respect of popularity. Not surprisingly, the Christians were in first place, but were represented by the numerous religions with their basis in Christianity. The fact that the census reported their following to be 37,046,500 compared to 32,404 Spiritualists gives you some indication as to how difficult it is for us to make our voice heard with any amount of respect.

ANTI-SPIRITUALISM

The majority of 'Spiritualism' character assassination comes from the Christian-based faiths, who base their anti-spiritualistic attitude on Bible quotations. However, the irony is; the Bible is full of psychic phenomena and Spirit communication. Many Spiritualists perceive the Bible as a spiritual guidebook to living and its inspiration for acts of psychic phenomena. We will take a critical look at some of the Christian arguments that are used to justify the condemnation and discrediting of our beliefs. In an attempt to highlight to the reader the inflexibility, inconsistency, injustice and lack of common sense used in the interpretation of the Bible. Just because someone of a different faith interprets the words and meaning of the Bible differently, does not mean they are in cahoots with Satan. Our point is that all paths lead to God and no single religion has the monopoly on God. A good example of this would be the Crusades, where both Christians and Muslims swore allegiance to God (although in different names), believed they had His support and sought victory on His behalf. During these times many used God as an excuse to gain status, power, land and wealth. And in His name millions died.

The Bible

Do Christians give any consideration to the age in which the writers of the books lived? How much of the authors' ancestral and philosophical beliefs, as well as social attitudes, were incorporated into their current belief system and as a result were reflected in the scriptures?

We ask the reader to consider who it was that decided which books/gospels should form part of what we know today as the Bible? Was it a case that the authors of the books put the Bible together to provide a natural progression or was there outside influence, such as the Council of Nicea? History records that various religious councils have been called at which the Bible has been 'moulded' into the format that we recognise today.

It seems logical to assume the Catholic Fathers of the time would select books that supported their current beliefs; a system that would also ensure their political power/influence. It also seems reasonable to assume they had to make sure their jobs were secure in the belief that the 'Priesthood' was needed in the community.

This of course poses the question; how much of the books of the Bible were edited or enhanced in order to ensure continual employment and re-enforcement of the religious interpretation of the time?

Today the Bible is open to many interpretations in accordance with the many Christian- based faiths that are in existence. They extract what they need to support their spiritual claims and ignore the rest. The Bible needs to be taken as a whole; if it is flawed in parts you cannot ignore it just because it does not suit you. The reader must ask why and how much of it is flawed. We believe the Bible is flawed because it is contradictory and although it is reputed to be the word of God, it was in fact not written by God but by Man. As such it has been manipulated by the religious councils through the years and possibly its original message lost or to the very least, obscured.

Today the Bible has become inflexible because devout followers take its meanings literally, including the flaws, and thus have not moved with the times. It was not meant to be taken as gospel (no pun intended!). However, the underlying message in the Bible behind such ideology as; thou shall not kill, love thy neighbour, looking beyond the physical person as Jesus taught and psychic phenomena, are all still very relevant today. The fact is, the Bible makes better sense when you interpret it from a Spiritualist's perspective.

Take for instance the very anti-Spiritualism website www.espministries.com. In the website's introduction the author ironically mentions that they at one time practiced Spiritualism, but does not appear to see fit to establish the reasons for their dramatic reversal of views. Unfortunately, whatever the circumstances, they seem to have taken it upon themselves to carry out a pious crusade to destroy the beliefs of those that still wish to follow Spiritualism.

The following extract is a good example of the typical argument from the anti-Spiritualists:

"We must never make the mistake of thinking that Spiritualism is dealing with fantasy or figments of people's imaginations. Spiritualism is real; it is a tool used by Satan to delude and captivate people's souls. The Bible strictly forbids God's people to deal with the spirit world (Deuteronomy 18:10; Leviticus 19:31, 20:6, 20:27; 1 Chronicles 10:13-14; 2 Kings 23:24; Isaiah 8:19-20). God would not forbid us to deal with something that did not exist. The religion deceives us by claiming to contact the dead; actually these contacts are demons who are impersonating the dead. Those practicing such divinations are actually violating the first command given by God - "You shall have no other gods before me" (Exodus 20:3) - and are encouraging demon activity. There is much danger inherent in such practices because of the result imbalance of the mind and soul when one allows demons to control his thoughts and actions."

The statement raises four poignant issues on which we would like to pass comment;

1. 'Spiritualism is real: it is a tool used by Satan to delude and captivate people's souls.'

The aim of Spiritualism is to be in service **to God**; to do good. We attempt to bring solace and upliftment through messages from Spirit and healing. Why would Satan bother to allow us to do this? Would he not prefer to see us causing pain and destruction? And even if this were true, why is it that Satan is so pro-active and God so passive; allowing Satan access to all the pertinent information required to impersonate a 'deceased' loved one?

> 2. 'God would not forbid us to deal with something
> that did not exist.'

The majority of Spiritualists believe in God and do a lot of good work in God's name. In that respect, we are no different from any other God-loving religions. We honestly believe that communicating with the 'dead' is God's wish and if this is so wrong, then why does God not correct us? After all, God is the all-knowing, all-caring, loving father. The reason God does not intervene and 'save' his Spiritualist children from the clutches of Satan, is because it is <u>not</u> the work of Satan and therefore God does not forbid it.

> 3. 'You shall have no other gods before me - and
> are encouraging demon activity.'

The implication here is that demons are gods, and as such worship demons as gods, and Spiritualists certainly do not believe demons are gods. To a Spiritualist, demons are those people who have 'died' and who did not lead a good, caring, kind life, and we term them 'negative' Spirit. Even they have the opportunity to use their freewill and to take responsibility for their actions; to lead a good, caring and kind existence even within the Spirit World.

> 4. 'There is much danger inherent in such practices
> because of the result imbalance of the mind and soul
> when one allows demons to control his thoughts and
> actions.'

The reality is that God gave Man freewill; freewill to do good or bad, freewill to speak with good or bad Spirits. It is our choice whether or not to take responsibility for our actions. As individuals it is our own level of spirituality and motives that will dictate the quality of Spirit that will subsequently make contact with us; like attracts like. And yes, the Medium's motives do count; are they selfless or egotistical, spiritual or materialistic?

When we 'die', we expect God to be there to guide us and not Satan, for we are good people and no different to those connected to espministries. The website also states:

> "Over the past 5,000 years history shows us that God closed the doors on 20 major civilisations when they permitted three things to happen;
> 1. Kill their children
> 2. Practice witchcraft
> 3. Tolerate homosexuality
> God then permitted that civilisation to be terminated."

Based on the views of www.espministries.com, we are therefore due for termination. Nothing like looking on the positive side! Of course the Christians were responsible for destroying a civilisation; the Inca civilisation springs to mind, because the Spanish Conquistador Pizarro and his men were driven by their greed for gold and wealth. How materialistic and un-spiritual is that? Did God authorise them to kill in his name? A loving God would not want to see his 'children' slaughtered in his name. So we ask the reader; would you want your children to torture and kill others in your name? NO. Neither does the Spiritualist's perception of God.

The need to make human and animal sacrifices is entrenched in those older civilisations who believed that gods were an extension of themselves and therefore were cannibals. How much of this is based on the distortion of ancient 'Spiritualism' is difficult to say. However, the need to make such sacrifices to appease the gods is even reflected in the Bible; with a prime example of child sacrifice being illustrated by God asking Abraham to sacrifice his own son, Isaac. Luckily for both Abraham and his son, God changed his mind. As a consequence, we wonder that if the God of the Bible is all-knowing and all-seeing, why did God not look into the heart and soul of Abraham and see the faith there? Instead God chose to test Abraham in a very cruel and heartless way. Why? Because the story was recounted based on primal beliefs of tribal sacrifice to appease the gods.

A time when sacrifices were made because the people believed the gods were cannibals like themselves, is expressed in how they worshipped. Today it is interesting to note that sacrifice still forms a basis of the Christian faith; God sacrificed his son Jesus, who died for our sins; the ultimate sacrifice <u>and</u> 'get out' clause for anyone who does not wish to take responsibility for their actions by repenting in the name of Jesus and the Almighty. As Christians they must often make a self sacrifice, but by doing so it does not necessarily make you a spiritual person.

There is a 'story' that best illustrates the difference between the Spiritualist attitude and that of members of other religions to personal sacrifice;

> A Spiritualist lady was conversing with a devout religious man who stated that he would die for 'his' God. The lady replied, "but my God would not ask me."

The author of www.espministries.com also believed that JK Rowling; the authoress of the 'Harry Potter' books, is corrupting the readers and has set the Christian Church back because of the witchcraft and spells contained in the storylines. Then again, in the 1950's people believed Elvis Presley was an evil/bad influence because of his gyrating movements on stage! Today no-one would blink an eye, for as times have changed so has morality and values too. So we ask, how far do you go before reason must occur?

Let's look at the biblical books mentioned by www.espministries.com, followed by our own interpretation;

1 Chronicles 10:13-14

[13] Saul died because he was unfaithful to the Lord; he did not keep the word of the Lord, and even consulted a medium for guidance, [14] and did not enquire of the Lord. So the Lord put him to death and turned the kingdom over to David son of Jesse.

Consulting with the Medium seems to have been added as an afterthought, the main point being that Saul was unfaithful and not concerned about the Lord. This has the undertones of a dictator who puts to death someone that disobeyed their instructions.

2 Kings 23:24

Furthermore, Josiah got rid of the mediums and spiritists, the household gods, the idols and all the other detestable things seen in Judah and Jerusalem. This he did to fulfil the requirements of the law written in the book that Hilkiah the priest had discovered in the temple of the Lord.

It is interesting to note that it seems Mediums and Spiritists were openly practising in Josiah's kingdom including Jerusalem, as too was the practice of worshiping other god/idols. The book of Kings also states that it was not until the eighteenth year of Josiah's reign that he received the book from Hilkiah. Why did the Priest wait so long before giving the King, God's written law or for God to have told him where to find the book if 'Spiritualism' was such a crime against the Lord? Why did God not intervene? If it was God's word, why did he not speak directly to Josiah, as seems to be the normal practice between God and the leaders in the Old Testament? Did the book contain the words of the Priests because they feared the popularity and ability of the Mediums and Spiritists?

In Isaiah, chapter 8, it states that the Lord spoke to him; was this clairaudiently? A mediumistic gift? Isaiah 8:13 also states that the Lord said:

> The Lord Almighty is the one you are to regard as
> holy, he is the one you are to fear, he is the one you
> are to dread,

God should not be feared by anyone, for according to the Christian faith, it is the Devil that is and should be feared. Which one should we consider is speaking to Isaiah? How did Isaiah know the difference, after all espministries tell us that demons impersonate the dead? So how do we know that Satan was not impersonating God in the case of Isaiah?

Christians automatically, and somewhat blindly, assume that the words in the Bible that are attributed to God, are in fact His words. Furthermore, they state that God is all-loving, all-knowing and dwells in love and light, and that it is the Devil/Satan who dwells in the darkness and the fires of Hell. If this is true, how then do they explain the circumstances surrounding Moses receiving the Ten Commandments and bearing in mind the aforementioned beliefs, what then was the true identity of the 'Lord' referred to in Deuteronomy 5:22?:

> [22] These are the commandments the Lord proclaimed
> in a loud voice to your whole assembly there on the

mountain from out of the fire, the cloud and the deep darkness;...

Isaiah 8:19-20

[19] When someone tells you to consult mediums and spiritists, who whisper and mutter, should not a people enquire of their God? Why consult the dead on behalf of the living? [20] To the law and to the testimony! If they do not speak according to this word, they have no light of dawn.

These verses show the extent to which the religious men believed that some would go to encourage/incite others to consult with mediums and spiritists, even suggesting direct communication with God was possible. However, the religious men countered by saying that it was against the religious law, was in effect blasphemy and those that chose that path would be in spiritual darkness.

Modern day Spiritualists do not claim to be in direct communication with God unlike all those religions created solely on the claims of their founders that God had spoken to them? Should more of the people have taken the opportunity, as some obviously did, to 'enquire of mediums and spiritists', we believe they would have discovered a God that does not instil fear, only love.

They ask, why consult the dead? The reality is that often it is Spirit who make initial contact to bring comfort to their love ones who grieve for them. People need actual proof that there is more than just the physical life.

The implication that Mediums and Spiritists are in spiritual darkness cannot be true because of the good works they strive to do in the name of God.

Leviticus 19:31

Do not turn to mediums or seek out spiritists, for you will be defiled by them. I am the Lord your God.

Leviticus 20:6

" 'I will set my face against all who turn to mediums and spiritists to prostitute themselves by following them, and I will cut them off from their people...' "

Leviticus 20:27

" 'A man or woman who is a medium or spiritist among you must be put to death. You are to stone them; their blood will be on their own heads.' "

According to Leviticus, God spoke to Moses; the reception of which, ironically, is a mediumistic ability in itself that contravenes the above. Bearing in mind this and other contradictions, just how seriously should one take the book of Leviticus? For instance, God gave Moses the Ten Commandments and yet in Leviticus 20:27 above, He is clearly encouraging people to break the 6th Commandment; You shall not murder, thus removing the responsibility away from the murderer(s).

Leviticus continues by keeping with the male orientated traditions of the day by quoting God as considering women to be unclean. This coming from the same God who had given women the ability to give birth after Eve's unfortunate incident with the apple in the garden of Eden:

Leviticus 12:2

...'A woman who becomes pregnant and gives birth

to a son will be ceremonially unclean for seven days, just as she is unclean during her monthly period.

And this stance continues with:

Leviticus 12:5-6

[5] If she gives birth to a daughter, for two weeks the woman will be unclean, as during her period. Then she must wait sixty-six days to be purified from her bleeding. [6] " 'When the days of her purification for a son or daughter are over, she is to bring to the priest at the entrance to the Tent of Meeting a year-old lamb for a burnt offering and a young pigeon or a dove for a sin offering.

If so many anti-Spiritualists quote Leviticus to condemn us, then why do they not make sacrifices as stated in Leviticus when they become parents? We are more civilised and wiser, and have outgrown this out-dated mode of thinking. Bringing children into the world is a beautiful thing, not an unclean act that requires purification. This attitude is totally out-dated, for nowadays parents celebrate such a wonderful event. In the same way the condemnation of Spiritualists is also out-dated, and as a result those that bring such judgement should move on and not select parts of the Bible merely to suit the needs of their argument; Spiritualism should also be celebrated.

Deuteronomy is considered one of the most important books in the Bible and it emphasises quite strongly what it considers 'Detestable Practices':

Deuteronomy 4:16

so that you do not become corrupt and make for

> yourselves an idol, an image of any shape, whether
> formed like a man or a woman,

With that in mind, answer this question: Why do Christians worship the image of Christ, Mary and the cross? Worship inflates the ego of the receiver, which would suggest that the God represented in the Bible is egotistical. Believing in and worshiping God are two very different aspects. The belief allows the individual to express reason and freewill, whereas worshipping can lead to dictatorship, obsession and fanaticism beyond reason.

> Deuteronomy 18:9-12

> [9] When you enter the land the Lord your God is giving you, do not learn to imitate the detestable ways of the nations there. [10] Let no-one be found among you who sacrifices a son or daughter in the fire, who practices divination or sorcery, interprets omens, engages in witchcraft, [11] or casts spells, or who is a medium or spiritist or who consults the dead. [12] Anyone who does these things is detestable to the Lord, and because of these detestable practices the Lord your God will drive out those nations before you.

Is it not totally hypocritical then that throughout the entire Bible there are numerous instances of some of the very same practices as mentioned above, all without condemnation? Joseph, in the book of Genesis, where he interprets the dreams (omens) of the Pharaoh, is actually rewarded and in fact he rose to become a good ruler of Egypt. Why did God favour Joseph if the act of divination was so detestable?

Even in later history the hypocrisy continued when the

religious men chose to ignore such direction as Deuteronomy 18:10, when during the witch hunts many 'sacrificed their daughters to the fire', with Joan of Arc being a prime example.

Are the words of Deuteronomy from God or merely the views of religious men of the time, who were trying to eradicate Paganism? We read in the Bible that God used prophets as a valuable source of imparting His laws to the people. So there were at least some 'mediumistic' prophets worthy of God's attention.

Today we can only 'judge' people by the driving force of their actions; to serve God and Mankind or to be greedy, selfish and arrogant. We wish to draw the attention of the reader to Deuteronomy 5:8-10, which is also the 2nd Commandment, as can be found in Exodus 20:4;

> [8] "You shall not make for yourself an idol in the form of anything in heaven above or on the earth beneath or in the waters below. [9] You shall not bow down to them or worship them; for I, the Lord your God, am a jealous God, punishing the children for the sin of the parents to the third and fourth generation of those who hate me, [10] but showing love to a thousand [generations] of those who love me and keep my commandments..."

God, as portrayed by those in the Spirit World, is not jealous or vengeful, but a God who is compassionate, just and cares about people irrespective of their religious beliefs, culture, gender, etc., because we are Spirit and thus spiritual beings. This is very different from the image Christians would have you believe; that the Spiritualist's God is in fact Satan. With reference to the above quote, which image does the word of God portray to you? If you are still not sure, maybe the following example of Saul, in the book of Samuel, can help you to decide:

1 Samuel 15:2-3

> [2] This is what the Lord Almighty says: 'I will punish the Amalekites for what they did to Israel when they waylaid them as they came up from Egypt. [3] Now go, attack the Amalekites and totally destroy everything that belongs to them. Do not spare them; put to death men and women, children and infants, cattle and sheep, camels and donkeys.'

God rejected Saul as King of Israel because he showed mercy and only destroyed all those that were despised and weak. Why did God not show mercy? What does that teach us spiritually? What does it teach our children? To be vengeful, merciless, cruel, violent, hateful. With this attitude on life, no wonder people, especially the younger generation, lack respect for most aspects of society. With this religious attitude, world peace will never be achieved. At this stage in our evolution, the God of the Bible has only himself to blame, since he created 'Man' in his own image; as one who is portrayed as vindictive and jealous.

If you choose to accept Leviticus and Deuteronomy, and readily condemn Spiritualists on face value, then reason would dictate that you must in turn accept Genesis, and Adam and Eve in the same way. To us this raises the following questions:

- If Adam and Eve were the only two, then where did Cain's wife come from?
- If Adam and Eve were the parents of Mankind, does this not insinuate relations of an incestial nature since Eve was the only woman and gave birth to Cain and Abel?

We cannot accept that an all-loving God would be an advocate of incestial relations. Is it not conceivable that God would have foreseen the need for a bigger gene pool? In the same way we find it difficult to believe that the same all-knowing, caring God would choose to put his 'beloved' children in an area where there was a snake; incidentally one that as later scripture testifies, must have originally been upright in stance or at least a biped.

God warns Adam and Eve about the tree of knowledge and then deliberately leaves them in the garden of Eden. This raises four questions:

1. Why deny Man the right to seek knowledge in the first place?
2. If eating from the tree of knowledge was forbidden why place Adam and Eve in the garden where they could be tempted? After all, God had created a universe and could have placed them anywhere.
3. Why did God, who is all-knowing, not know what was happening in his garden?
4. God must have known about the existence of the 'snake'; who was intelligent and at least a biped, yet He did not take appropriate action to expel the snake from the garden?

A good father, a good parent, would protect their children and as such God failed miserably. If the God of the Bible is as forgiving as he is portrayed, He should have taken responsibility for His actions and given Adam and Eve a second chance. Instead he chose to take it out on Mankind as portrayed in the Bible. It only serves to invoke the saying; 'Practice what you preach'. If the Adam and Eve story is considered merely symbolic, then how can we consider the likes of Leviticus and Deuteronomy to be the words of God and the condemnation of Spiritualism justified? Whatever biblical quotation is used by anti-Spiritualists, it can be challenged by Spiritualists with others, because the Bible is a matter of interpretation. You only have to look at the number of different Christian-based religions there are, all believing that their God is the one true God.

The book of Luke in the Bible gives us an insight into the

Pharisees' self perception; one of spiritual superiority. So imagine how the Pharisees and Jews perceived Jesus. Here was a young, and probably charismatic man, a nobody, uneducated to their standard, telling them they have got their religion wrong. To rub salt in the wound, this man lived what he 'preached'; he associated with lepers, harlots and the 'unclean'. Jesus did not have social standing, was considered uncultured and lacked the necessary ecclesiastical traditions. Jesus supported his claims through what we classify today as psychic phenomena.

Jesus broke Hebrew Law by openly 'consorting' with Spirit both good and bad, as the following examples show:

Jesus drove two demons into a herd of pigs that ran into and drowned in a lake, while those tending the pigs ran off to the town to report the events.

> Matthew 8:34
>
> Then the whole town went out to meet Jesus. And when they saw him, they pleaded with him to leave their region.

Why plead with Jesus? Was it because they were scared of him for consorting with demons, or because of the risk of any religious recriminations if they had done nothing?

And Jesus had other dealings with the demon-possessed;

> Matthew 9:32-34
>
> [32] While they were going out, a man who was demon-possessed and could not talk was brought to Jesus. [33] And when the demon was driven out, the man who had been mute spoke. The crowd was amazed

> and said, "Nothing like this has ever been seen in Israel." [34] But the Pharisees said, "It is by the prince of demons that he drives out demons."

This is a bit reminiscent of the anti-relationship that Christians have with Spiritualists. In standing and power, the Christian faith is the equivalent to the Jewish faith at the time of the Bible. The Jews perceived Jesus to be consorting with Satan (the 'Prince of demons'), which in essence is no different to the Christian faith accusing Spiritualists of consorting with demons. If nowadays it is accepted that Jesus was not in fact consorting with demons, then why is it wrong for Spiritualists? Many Christian followers try to emulate Jesus by incorporating his teachings into their lives, so why is it not acceptable for Spiritualists to do the same with regards to the psychic phenomena that he and his disciples accomplished?

Jesus gave authority to his twelve disciples to heal, and drive out demons;

> Matthew 10:8

> Heal the sick, raise the dead, cleanse those who have leprosy, drive out demons. Freely you have received, freely give.

Surely to raise the dead is necromancy and against the teachings of the Old Testament. To make matters worse, Jesus is inciting his disciples to practice necromancy as well! If Jesus and his disciples had been alive and practicing during the witch hunts of the 15th to 18th centuries, they would have been burnt alive, thus experiencing the same fate as Joan of Arc; who incidentally was a 'Medium' but is now a Saint! Perhaps as Spiritualists we should adopt Joan of Arc as our Saint!

Here is a different thought perspective to consider; Genesis states that God created Man in his own image. We interpret this as meaning in the form of 'Spirit' and not with regards to physical appearance. The quote in Luke 17:21 which states; "...the kingdom of God is within you", clearly refers to the Spirit within the physical body and those Spiritualists who opt for a more Christian-based belief system, and as such recognise the existence of the trinity, term this the Holy Spirit.

God in his infinite wisdom gave Man the ability to talk to Him by means of psychic ability, often sending Messengers/ Angels in the form of Spirit, but Man in his greed for power and self-arrogance has failed to accept this fact. If God is our Father, as stated in the Bible, how else is the Father going to communicate with his children? God gave Man the ability for telepathy; to be guided and inspired by those in the Spirit World who are in continual service to God.

Jesus questioned the Jewish people's continued denial of the truth when he spoke to them concerning his relationship to Abraham;

John 8:46-47

"...[46] Can any of you prove me guilty of sin? If I am telling the truth, why don't you believe me?
[47] Whoever belongs to God hears what God says. The reason you do not hear is that you do not belong to God."

Later the Jews countered with;

John 8:52-53

[52] ..."Now we know that you are demon-possessed! Abraham died and so did the prophets, yet you say

that whoever keeps your word will never taste death. [53] Are you greater than our father Abraham? He died, and so did the prophets. Who do you think you are?"

Jesus contested the point with them further;

John 8:55-59

"...[55] Though you did not know him, I know him. If I said I did not, I would be a liar like you, but I do know him and keep his word. [56] Your father Abraham rejoiced at the thought of seeing my day; he saw it and was glad." [57] "You are not yet fifty years old," the Jews said to him, "and you have seen Abraham!" [58] "I tell you the truth," Jesus answered, "before Abraham was born, I am!" [59] At this, they picked up stones to stone him, but Jesus hid himself, slipping away from the temple grounds.

Again John re-iterates that people thought that Jesus had a link/connection with demons, but Jesus defends himself in 8:55 by indicating that he knew Abraham from the Spirit World since Abraham had physically died. This statement is re-enforced in 8:56 when it is inferred that Abraham gave his blessing to the incarnation of Jesus to his people. In 8:58 Jesus states that he was alive before Abraham was born into the physical body, both being non-corporeal beings (Spirit). Finally in 8:59 the Jews attempt to stone Jesus because of the heresy spoken. This action is very symbolic of the argument used by today's Christians against Spiritualists; communication with the dead, as Jesus had done with Abraham, is considered the work of the Devil.

Jesus could recognise 'demons' and more to the point, exorcise them. Christians today would argue that he was the Son of God and a part of the trinity, but during Jesus' time the Pharisees and

Jews did not think he was the 'Messiah'. To them he was a man who clearly consorted with demons/familiar Spirits and therefore must have contravened Leviticus and Deuteronomy. In fact John tells the reader how Jesus just narrowly missed being stoned - which incidentally was also the punishment for acts of 'Spiritism'. As Spiritualists we try to emulate him by healing the sick, practicing tolerance and acceptance for all, and using our psychic abilities to help others in the name of God.

The Complete Bible Handbook (pg 378), on the subject of Magic in the Bible, which can relate to divination, necromancy, exorcism, witchcraft and astrology, states;

> "The basic point is that any practices associated with
> magic are condemned if they detract from trust and
> faith in God."

The majority of Spiritualists have faith in God; a faith that strongly believes that 'God' will protect 'His' children when linking with the Spirit World. Spiritualists open their services with prayer; seeking and asking 'God' for guidance and protection, and for all links made with the Spirit World to be done in love, light, truth and with God's blessing. As Spiritualists we seek counsel with Spirits that are termed as 'God's Messengers/Angels', but we prefer to call them Spirit Guides/Helpers, sent to connect both worlds in love, peace and harmony.

We can sympathise with Jesus because through his teachings he was trying to inspire people to rethink their understanding and perception of God; what people could achieve by using their latent psychic abilities; "if you believe in me, you can be like me", and for this he was slandered as a heretic. Spiritualists today have to contend with not only slander but libellous statements. Mind you, this is less painful than being stoned, burnt as a witch or even crucified!

Spiritualists believe Jesus was a Medium and that he defied the orthodox religion of the time who believed that they were the <u>one</u> true religion. Jesus confronted their beliefs by consorting with 'demons', for he recognised that it was a natural part of life and not to be feared. He proved that the 'demon' could be removed from having its mental hold on an individual. Jesus did not say to the people pray to the Father God and the demon will depart, but instead took positive action, aided by the fact he could differentiate between good and bad Spirits.

The Bible is a guidebook to spiritual living/a philosophy on life, with God as the spiritual mentor/the spiritual perfection/the unconditional love that Mankind is trying to achieve. We believe that you should be free to take what you want from the Bible, but not to use its contents as a 'tool'/'weapon' to condemn others. Such actions are neither spiritual nor worthy of a God that is spiritual perfection and shows unconditional love to all his children, no matter what spiritual pathway they follow. Do not be unwilling advocates for the Christian Devil by spreading fear because of a different belief structure.

It is not the belief in God that has cost thousands of millions of lives in our world history, but the religious men who instilled fear into the people in order to control them and the kings who permitted this to happen as a means of preventing anarchy. It just boils down to the desire for power; not just in the case of control, but also over life and death. Then there was the aspect of greed and the desire for status that the power and wealth could bring. Symbolically this drive for power and control in all aspects of life is the biggest 'devil' known to Man.

Spiritualists would neither threaten nor implement the use of imprisonment and/or torture in order to either achieve our aims or force our beliefs upon others. Though we accept that we may not be immune to the odd fanatic, we are proud of the fact that we can, and do, embrace diversity in accordance with belief and religious freedom. These are certainly not the values of the Devil, unless of course you belief that democracy and the value of life are works of the Devil also.

Let us assume for a moment that the Spiritualists are wrong and the Christians are right; there is no Spirit World. Upon resurrection and Judgement Day, what would God say to us as Spiritualists? Would He say, "You communicated with 'demons' that encouraged you to do good acts in my name, but you never hurt anyone, you cared and tried your best to be a good person. You were under the false illusion those 'demons' were sent by me as my representatives, but you were wrong. Should I, as the kind, caring, loving God you believe me to be, allow you into my 'Kingdom of Heaven'? Or shall I be an unmerciful, unforgiving, uncaring God (exhibiting traits of the Devil/Zeus) and condemn you to Hell?"

Logic, reason and faith tells us that God would not punish the Spiritualists unjustly. He would look right into their hearts and souls, recognise the type of person they are and whether good or bad, would pass judgement accordingly.

HISTORY
OF
SPIRITUALISM

The birth of gods

Spiritualism, insomuch as a belief in communication with Spirit, is probably the oldest religion and has existed in one form or another throughout Mankind's history. In antiquity it was in the guise of Oracles and Shamanism before Modern Spiritualism started in 1848, in the USA. Incidentally, the Mormon faith began earlier in 1830, but the Jehovah's Witnesses faith was founded later in 1872. It was proposed by Arthur Findlay in 'The Rock of Truth' that Spiritualism was actually the parent of religion; the act of worshipping god(s).

Findlay further proposed that as Primitive Man developed intellectually and became more inquisitive, he questioned his surroundings and the role of the natural elements within it. In time, Primitive Man recognised loved ones and friends that had 'died' and subsequently linked 'Spirit' sightings with certain events/situations in their daily life. People then began asking these Spirits to bring good fortune to the family and community; the instigation of prayer. This naturally progressed to the creation of effigies which they began to worship, forgetting their origins and what they represented. The result was the 'birth' of gods.

Aided by the fact that Primitive Man would not have had writing skills, stories of psychic experiences were passed down in the form of verbal stories from generation to generation and as such were open to exaggeration; an extreme case of 'Chinese Whispers'. All this contributed to the powers and personality traits they believed the gods possessed.

Sacrifices

Early primitive 'Priesthoods' often practiced cannibalism and logically reasoned, albeit incorrectly, that because Spirit was an extension of themselves, the gods were also cannibals. Therefore sacrifices were needed to appease the gods and get them to act favourably for numerous purposes; to make the crops grow, change fortunes, the sun to rise, etc. Even today we can see the interpretation that God is an extension of Man, because it states in the Bible, 'God made man in His own image'.

The Holy place became the sacrificial altar. Priests ate the flesh and drunk the blood which represented life, hence both became sacred. This was also portrayed in the representation given in the Gospels of the Last Supper, where the drinking of the wine and eating of the bread represented the blood and flesh of Christ.

The introduction of the Halo

It would seem logical to assume that if Primitive Man was psychically active; could 'see' the Spirits of the departed, then it would be recorded in the art and stories of the time.

He would have been able to discern the energy around the crown of the Medium as a result of Spirit activity. Mediums were the link to the Spirit World and the 'gods', and thus the people would have perceived the energy of light/the glow as associated with Spiritual beings.

Arthur Findlay tells us in the 'The Rock of Truth' (pg 15);

> "The halo, which is seen around some Mediums, was transformed into a golden orb like the sun, and the saviour-gods were depicted with the Sun behind their heads."

When you look at some of the religious-based paintings and sculptures, the religious figure will often have a disc/halo behind them and generally these figures are associated with 'Heaven' and the afterlife (see figs. 1 - 3).

The halo described by Arthur Findlay reminded us of a visit to the Nazca Lines in Peru in 1989 and the photographs taken from a light aircraft of the figure described as an 'astronaut' (see fig. 4). Interestingly, not only the 'astronaut' but all the drawings/ lines/geometric shapes on the plains, are only clearly visible from the air. You could therefore interpret the figure, not as an alien from the skies as suggested by Erich von Daniken's theory, but as 'Spirit' from the 'Heavens'. Whatever the truth may be, the Nazca Lines are an amazing accomplishment considering they are thought to date from the 6th C AD. Doesn't it make you wonder where they derived their inspiration from?

Fig. 1 - image taken from Kykkos Monastery, Cyprus 2004

Fig. 2 - image taken from above an exterior door of Salisbury Cathedral 2005
(note the discs behind each head)

Fig. 3 - An unused church in Göreme, Turkey

Fig. 4 - The 'Astronaut' of the Nazca Lines, Peru
(as viewed from an aeroplane)

The Oracle of Delphi

Delphi was located on the slopes of Mount Parnassus, in Greece, which was believed at the time to be the centre of the Earth. It was so popular that people from as far as Egypt, Asia Minor and Italy would travel to see the Oracle; a Trance Medium known as the Pythia, and speak with Spirit. Before the 'Medium' spoke, sacrificial rituals were performed during which time the enquirer would write their question. The 'Priest' would then obtain the answer from the entranced Medium and interpret the words spoken. Often Kings and Generals would consult the Oracle before making major decisions.

> "Delphi owed its fame to the oracles delivered by the Pythia, who received direct inspiration from Apollo and spoke in his name; in other words, the god of divination himself delivered the oracle, using the Pythia as a medium."
> [The Greek Museums: Delphi, Ekdotike Athenon S.A.]

The people of the time actually believed that the god Apollo spoke through the Medium to the people, just as the God of the Bible had spoken to Moses, Abraham and others in the Old Testament. The people believed Apollo, as a god, broke his own law and exiled himself from Delphi for eight years until he had made amends for his actions. Although their gods (in reality, Spirit) were believed to be an extension of themselves, they were considered omnipotent, with seemingly 'supernatural' powers, but not above the law. The gods were flawed, imperfect, just as Spirit. Today, seeing and hearing Spirit forms a part of psychic phenomena, so in reality what Primitive Man worshipped was in fact psychic phenomena. It was something seemingly supernatural to them, which they attributed to Spirit and as a result Spirit emerged as gods.

Delphi was systematically destroyed by the Roman Christian Emperors, as was the relationship between Priest and Medium. It seems Delphi always 'employed' the Medium but many other oracles were not as fortunate, often becoming the victim of the unscrupulous.

The Priest protected the sacred place and ensured the rituals were carried out, but in time the relationship between Priest and Medium ceased because the Priest realised that he could mimic the Medium convincingly enough to deceive the people, thus in essence becoming the 'Oracle of the gods'. This is reflected throughout our history; religious men/leaders claiming that they are the spokespersons for God.

The website www.dreamscape.com informs the reader that since 1932 it has been known that the High Priestess of Rome, 'Cumaean Sibyl' and others delivered the oracles whilst in a trance state:

> "The Cumaean Sibyl was especially venerated by early Christians not only for her prophetic gift but also because she had specifically prophesized the birth of Christ - the fact of which most of today's Christians remain unaware."

It is believed the Pythia spoke her last words as the Oracle of Delphi to Emperor Julian the Apostate (c.331-363). It is interesting to note that the Pythia was always female, as is the case today with the majority of Mediums and Psychics.

The Nechung State Oracle

The people of traditional Tibet were often Mediums or Healers, and the monasteries all had protective deities. The most successful deity was the Nechung State Oracle and the prophecies of this protective deity have played an important part in Tibetan history.

Buddhism is one of the few religions that do not believe in an omnipotent god, although as stated they do believe that certain deities connected with their belief act solely as protectors. It has been recorded that from 1642 the Nechung State Oracle has been regularly consulted as is still the case even today. The Dalai Lama; the spiritual leader of Tibet and his Government; the Kashag, consult Spirit in the form of the Nechung State Oracle twice a year seeking guidance and advice on such topics as political and state issues. The Nechung is even consulted with regards to the names of boys that are potential candidates as the reincarnation of the next Dalai Lama.

A monk, known as the Kuten, acts as a Medium. Dressed in colourful ceremonial gowns weighing in excess of 70lbs, topped off with a special helmet that alone weighs 30lbs, he performs traditional prayers and rituals conducive to him sliding slowly deeper into a trance. Once in trance, the Medium is controlled by an ancient protective deity known as Dorje Drakden; a pre-Buddhist demon said to have been tamed and converted by the Indian guru, Padmasambhava. Despite the heaviness of his regalia, he dances around often thrashing a heavy sword above his head, prostrates himself and makes offerings to the Dalai Lama before taking his place on a stool in order to take any questions from both the Dalai Lama and the members of the Kashag.

After booming out his surprisingly precise answers to the questions, the Oracle dances again, gives a final offering to the Dalai Lama, before falling still and lifeless to the floor, signalling an end to the control. The heavy helmet is quickly removed to save the Medium from throttling himself under the weight and he is then carried away to recover fully in private.

The official website of the government of Tibet in exile, www.tibet.com, states that his Holiness the Dalai Lama writes in his autobiography 'Freedom in Exile':

> "For hundreds of years now, it has been traditional
> for the Dalai Lama, and the Government, to consult

Nechung during the New Year festivals. In addition, he might well be called upon at other times if either have specific queries…….. This is not to say that I rely solely on the oracle's advice. I do not. I seek his opinion in the same way as I seek the opinion of my Cabinet and just as I seek the opinion of my conscience. I consider the gods to be my 'upper house'. The Kashag constitutes my 'lower house'. Like any other leader, I consult both before making a decision on affairs of state. And sometimes, in addition to Nechung's counsel, I also take into consideration certain prophecies."

This well respected religion uses numerous methods of divination to not only foretell the future but also to guide the user to answers concerning illnesses and other problems. Such methods include;

- Dough ball, dice, rosary, bootstraps, mirror, shoulder blade, and hearing divinations.
- The interpretation of incidental signs, dreams, and flames.
- The observing of a butter lamp.

All are recognisable as forms used in the West, or at least resemble them in some way, and as such clearly indicate how similar and intertwined psychic methods are despite the cultural differences.

This highlights the point we wish to make clear to all those who believe that all communication and direction given by Spirit is faultless, infallible. This is simply not true. As with the Dalai Lama, all information received should be accepted as merely guidance or opinion. Spirit Guides do not and should not dictate, for you have the freewill to take their counsel, their advice, or not. Whatever your choice, the decision and its outcome is your responsibility, not Spirit's. We also believe this freedom from responsibility extends to God, for despite our tendency to apportion blame elsewhere, the fault lies ultimately with Man and not God. We have freewill and often choose to ignore responsibility because it is inconvenient.

Shamanism

Even today Shamanism is practiced around the world, and is particularly popular with the Native American Indians, as well as in Northern Asia and Africa. As the spiritual leader, the Shaman (priest, medicine man, seer, prophet, etc.), has the responsibility of linking their society/community to the Spirit World. The people expect the Shaman to control both good and evil Spirits and to cure illnesses with his 'special powers' (psychic abilities). Again this occurs in a trance state and the spiritual leader; the Shaman, is the 'Medium'. Often the Shaman uses 'drugs' to induce a trance state whereas Spiritualists need only a meditative quietening of the mind.

> ... The traditional image of the European witch on her broom stick [see chapter illustration for 'History of Spiritualism'] is believed to be a metaphor for shamanic flight, in which the shaman's spirit leaves his or her physical body and travels the world and the realm of the spirits.
>
> [The Illustrated Encyclopaedia of Divination]

THE AGE OF THE GREEK PHILOSOPHERS

Pythagoras (c.580-500 BC)

He trained with Egyptian Priests in his early years and was the first to suggest that the Earth was spherical and orbited the Sun. However, despite this he is best remembered as a mathematician; Pythagoras' theorem. He was a firm believer in reincarnation and claimed he could remember his past lives.

Herodotus (c.484-424 BC)

Considered the first historian after he wrote a nine-book history of the Greek-Persian struggle. The website www.williamjames.com relates from the writings of Herodotus that the King of Lydia, Croesus, sent messengers to the various oracles to test them. It was agreed that on the hundredth day after their departure they would ask the Oracle what Croesus was doing at that very moment. Upon entering the temple of Delphi and before the emissaries could pose their question the Priestess told them the answer to their as yet unasked question. They recorded the communication and Croesus was so impressed by the accuracy he sent presents to Delphi of incalculable value.

Socrates (c.470-399 BC)

In his book 'Phaedo', Plato relates to the conversation that Socrates has with Cebes and Simmias prior to his committing suicide by drinking hemlock:

> "It is right to think then, gentlemen that if the soul is immortal, it requires our care not only for the time we call our life, but for the sake of all time, and that one is in terrible danger if one does not give it that care. If death were escape from everything, it would be a great boon to the wicked to get rid of the body and of their wickedness together with their soul. But now that the soul appears to be immortal, there is no escape from evil or salvation for it except by becoming as good and wise as possible, for the soul goes to the underworld possessing nothing but its education and upbringing, which are said to bring the greatest benefit or harm to the dead right at the beginning of the journey yonder."

> "We are told that when each person dies the guardian spirit who was allotted to him in life proceeds to lead him to a certain place, whence those who have been gathered together there must, after being judged, proceed to the underworld with the guide who has been appointed to lead them thither from here. Having there undergone what they must and stayed there the appointed time, they are led back here by another guide after long periods of time...."

[Classics of Western Philosophy]

In Plato's 'Apology', Xenophon attributes the following words to Socrates:

> "This prophetic voice has been heard by me throughout my life: it is certainly more trustworthy than omens from the flight or entrails of birds: I call it a God or daemon [demigod and not an evil demon]. I have told my friends the warnings I have received, and up to now the voice has never been wrong."

[www.williamjames.com]

Although we do not believe you go to the underworld (Hell), you have to take into consideration the era in which Socrates lived, as well as the spiritual beliefs of the times being based upon the Greek gods of Olympus (Heaven) and Hades (Hell). What you have is in fact Socrates' attempt to explain Spiritualism in terms of Greek mythology; to, if you will, combine the two. Just as Christian Spiritualists combine their belief of a Spirit World and the teachings of Jesus.

It is not clear how the word 'demon' came to be associated with evil beings. The original spelling was 'daemon' meaning demigod and guardian spirit of a place or person. This would indicate that the demon initially represented good, but at Christianity's conception all that was not within their belief system was tainted as pagan and therefore negative or evil. In their attempt to eradicate anything of a pagan nature, they carried out what could only be described as a character assassination on the 'daemon'/demon. In this respect, we can look at the word 'devil' to understand how time and beliefs can corrupt terminology:

> "...early books of the Old Testament, it was God who inflicted punishment on men, while one of his officials – known as 'the satan', Hebrew for 'adversary' – acted as a prosecutor."
>
> [Reader's Digest; Illustrated Dictionary of Essential Knowledge, pg 79]

To further support the belief that the use of the term Satan/The Devil has been corrupted beyond all recognition over time, we need look no further than the words of Jesus himself when speaking to Peter, as referred to in Matthew 16:23;

> "Get behind me Satan! You are a stumbling-block to me; you do not have in mind the things of God, but the things of men."

Jesus considered Peter his adversary because he stood up against his views and could only see the outcome of events ahead from a physical and not a spiritual perspective. If Jesus considered Peter to be Satan in the way we understand the term today, then why did the Church credit Peter as the first Pope of Rome?

A classic example of how images can be distorted for one reason or another is that of Jesus. It seems unbelievable to consider that the very same Jesus, so revered today as the law of love, service and sacrifice, was called the 'prince of devils' 2,000 years ago. The Pharisees and Jews looked upon him as a man that stirred up trouble. They called him, "a friend of Beelzebub, a friend of sinners and a wine bibber."

Democritus (c.460-361 BC)

Produced the theory on the atomic structure of the universe which has contributed significantly to metaphysics.

> "At death, Democritus maintained in a book called Chirokmeta, that soul molecules detach themselves from the corpse, thus giving rise to spectres."
>
> [www.williamjames.com]

Democritus was trying to explain the existence of the soul after death and he also believed the following to be true:

> "….that objects of all sorts, and especially people continually emitted what he termed images – particles on the atomic level that carried representations of the mental activities, thoughts, characters and emotions of the persons who originated them. 'And thus charged, they have the effect of living agents: by their impact they could communicate and transmit to their recipients the opinions, thoughts, and impulses of their senders, when they reach their goal with the images intact and undistorted'. The images 'which leap out from persons in an excited and inflamed condition', yield, owing to their high frequency and rapid transit, especially vivid and significant representations."
>
> [www.williamjames.com]

This is an excellent example of an individual trying to explain the 'psychic imprint' left on objects that Psychics are able to read and the existence of the lifeforce as pure thought energy.

Plato (c.428-347 BC)

A pupil of Socrates, his philosophy has had an influence upon Christianity and European culture, as well as philosophical topics on metaphysics, ethics and politics. He believed in reincarnation, that the soul continued its existence after death, and endured many incarnations to obtain spiritual perfection. Plato believed that although the Soul was linked to the body it was also linked to God; the soul belonged to the 'spiritual world' and the human body to the 'material world'. This belief is reflected in Plato's works entitled the 'Republic' and 'Gorgias'.

Spirit tell us that we are not meant to remember past lives or our Spirit life before reincarnating, to avoid flooding our mind with memories and thoughts from a past that we no longer have an influence upon. The purpose of our earthly existence is first and foremost to re-discover our spiritual existence; a spiritual awakening. Then armed with this knowledge, to achieve successful completion of the lessons for which we incarnated. It was therefore interesting to discover that Plato taught the following:

> "That before each incarnation, the soul enters into a forgetfulness of what has gone before. The purpose of human learning and philosophy is, then, to reawaken in the soul remembrance of the eternal, spiritual realm of pure forms and ideas."
>
> [www.williamjames.com]

The same website informs us that Socrates too had a perceptive explanation of what death is:

> "death, as it seem to me, is actually nothing but the disconnection of two things, the soul and the body, from each other."

Stefan Stenudd's article, 'Cosmos of the Ancients; The Greek

Philosophers on Myths and Cosmology', quotes Plato from 'Gorgias':

> "Zeus decided that they should be judged after death, when bodies and souls were separated from each other and naked, completely revealed. People also had to be ignorant of the time of their death, so that they would be unprepared."

[www.stenudd.com]

As Spiritualists, we know that when we leave the Physical World to join the Spirit World, we are in essence naked, not physically but as a Spirit being. We cannot hide from who we are; the façade has gone and there is no escaping the wrongs we have committed, no matter how trivial they were. We are faced literally with the naked truth and many of us will not like what we see.

Euhemerus (c.330-260 BC)
Believed 'gods' were originally living men and elevated through fear, wealth, power, etc. Christianity has a similar concept in Christ; an ordinary man elevated to god-like status. Euhemerus' theory is interesting, because if Primitive Man saw the Spirit of those they knew and who had 'died', it is feasible that after generations facts would become distorted and myths are born. We can see the traits of Man such as fear, theft, adultery and deceit in the Greek gods. For instance Zeus was reported to have eaten his first wife who was pregnant with Athena, just in case his daughter may have become more powerful than him.

As with Primitive Man, the Greeks perceived their gods to be extensions of themselves reflecting all aspects of human nature, although they believed they also possessed supernatural powers and were omnipotent. This image is clearly reflected in the God of the Holy Bible. At times he is portrayed as kind, all-loving, then smiting down people and nations, not dissimilar to Zeus.

St. Paul (c.3 BC-68 AD)
Christian missionary and martyr, originally known as Saul of
Tarsus. As the author of Corinthians 1 & 2 in the Bible, he speaks
of gifts of the Spirit:

> 1 Corinthians 12:7-11

> [7] Now to each one the manifestation of the Spirit is
> given for the common good. [8] To one there is given
> through the Spirit the message of wisdom, to another
> the message of knowledge by means of the same
> Spirit, [9] to another faith by the same Spirit, to another
> gifts of healing by that one Spirit, [10] to another
> miraculous powers, to another prophecy, to another
> distinguishing between spirits, to another speaking
> in different kinds of tongues, and to still another
> the interpretation of tongues. [11] All these are the work
> of one and the same Spirit, and he gives them to
> each one, just as he determines.

St. Paul states:

> 1 Corinthians 12:28

> And in the church God has appointed first of all
> apostles, second prophets, third teachers, then
> workers of miracles, also those having gifts of
> healing, those able to help others, those with gifts
> of administration, and those speaking in different
> kinds of tongues.

St. Paul knew and recognised the existence of Spirit and the
psychic abilities people possessed that allowed them to
communicate with Spirit and vice versa. He came to believe,

as we do now, that all paths lead to God. This is supported in 1 Corinthians 12:4-6:

> [4] There are different kinds of gifts, but the same Spirit. [5] There are different kinds of service, but the same Lord. [6] There are different kinds of working, but the same God works all of them in everyone.

Origen of Alexandria (c. 185/6 - 254/5 AD)

Was the first systematic theologian and philosopher of the Christian Church and was well respected as a spiritual teacher during his lifetime. He incorporated the teachings of Plato into his Christian beliefs which included the pre-existence of souls, their subsequent restoration to a purely intellectual existence, and the freedom of each and every soul. Origen's primary belief was that of reincarnation.

He believed that God initially created rational beings, that through contemplation due to their close proximity to God, spiritually speaking, could learn about the divine mysteries. Eventually these souls grew tired of constant contemplation and began to move away from God. The only soul that remained true to God was the 'soul of Christ'.

> "What are now souls began as *minds*, and through boredom or distraction grew 'cold' as they moved away from the 'divine warmth'. Thus departing from God, they came to be clothed in bodies, at first of a 'fine ethereal and invisible nature,' but later, as souls fell further away from God, their bodies changed 'from a fine, ethereal and invisible body' to a body of a coarser and more solid state. The purity of the body with which a soul is enveloped depends upon the moral development and perfection of the soul to which it is joined. Origen states that there are varying

degrees of subtleness even among the celestial and spiritual bodies. When a soul achieves s a l v a t i o n, according to Origen, it ceases being a soul, and returns to a state of pure 'mind' or *understanding.* However, due to the fall, now 'no rational spirit can ever exist without a body' but the bodies of redeemed souls are 'spiritual bodies', made of the purest fire."

[www.reluctant-messenger.com]

So if we were to apply Origen's theory to Adam and Eve in Genesis; once they became self aware and distanced themselves from God the divine, they eventually developed solid form. In effect Adam and Eve heralded the beginning of Spirit expressing itself through a physical body, and the start of Mankind's journey to rediscover its spiritual and divine heritage with God. The good news is; God does not abandon Adam and Eve, or Mankind, because upon the death of their physical body they return back to Him as pure intelligence; thought. Thus the Spirit returns home and has the freewill to choose whether or not to incarnate for further spiritual experiences.

"This is accomplished through education of souls who, having fallen away from God, are now sundered from the divine presence and require a gradual re-initiation into the mysteries of God. Such a reunion must not be accomplished by force, for God will never, Origen insists, undermine the free will of his creatures; rather, God will, over the course of numerous ages if need be, educate souls little by little, leading them eventually, by virtue of their own growing responsiveness, back to himself, where they will glory in the uncovering of the infinite mysteries of the eternal godhead."

[www.reluctant-messenger.com]

The Council of Nicea 325 AD

A Libyan Priest called Arius, believed Christ was not the son of God because Christ had a beginning but became God's son in human form. This view upset Bishop Alexander of Alexandria because the implication was that everyone was a child of God, making Jesus the same as you and I, and as such not unique. In an attempt to settle the argument, the Roman Emperor Constantine convened the Council in Bithynia (now Isnik, Turkey). Among a total of 318 Christian Fathers in attendance, there was only a token representation from the West.

The political and employment advantage to the Fathers was to declare that the human soul is unique to the Physical World and does not have a pre-existence. Thus the soul requires salvation through the Church for the soul has never been a part of God, the belief being that God creates souls at the point of conception.

The heated debate of what became known as the 'Arian controversy', which had split the Church in 320 AD, finally ended with the Council rejecting Arius' philosophy which had posed a serious threat to Christian beliefs as we know them today. This was the turning point for Christianity, for now the Fathers had the full support of the Roman Emperor Constantine who declared Christianity to be the official religion of the Roman Empire. The outcome was that the 'Nicene Creed' was born; 'the Son was one in being with the Father'. This in effect signalled the demise of Spiritualism and the rejection of Origen's teachings; that the soul has a beginning, is eternal, it has an innate ability of spiritual awareness, freewill and the opportunity to incarnate numerous times, to aid spiritual progression ultimately leading to the soul rejoining with God.

We do not believe it was erroneous of Emperor Constantine to make Christianity the religion of the Roman Empire, because it brought about an end to the persecution of so many Christians that lost their lives under the reign of numerous previous emperors. What was in fact erroneous was the Council's perception of human beings and their souls in relation to God, not to mention Constantine's switching his attention to the persecution of the Arians instead.

The sad irony is that in subsequent centuries Christianity in essence, replaced the Roman Empire and became the persecutor in its attempt to 'conquer' people by religious conversion and to eradicate anything that opposed or threatened their status, power and beliefs.

2nd Council of Constantinople 553 AD

Those Bishops who were anti-Origenism disagreed with Origen's belief of the pre-existence of souls and the resurrection of the dead. They refused to believe that the body returns to dust and that the Spirit, expressing itself through the physical body, is 'resurrected'; released to join with God, and that spiritual progression is achieved through reincarnation.

> "Origen was a person devoted to scriptural authority, a scourge to the enemies of the Church, and a martyr for the faith. He was the Spiritual teacher of a large and grateful posterity and yet his teachings were declared heresy in 553."
>
> [www.reluctant-messenger.com]

Genocide (c.1450-1750)

The genocide period of Europe is better known as the witch hunts and it is difficult for historians to confirm an accurate figure for men and women who lost their lives during that period. Brain Levack's book 'The Witch-Hunt in Early Modern Europe' states:

> "...[Levack] surveyed regional studies and found that there were approximately 110,000 witch

trials...... On average, 48% of trials ended in an execution, [and] therefore he estimated 60,000 witches died."

[www.genocide.org]

These figures are slightly higher than Robin Brigg's calculation in 'Witches and neighbours' (pg 8) in order to allow for the above average numbers of witch killings in Germany, believed to be the centre of persecution in Europe:

"...most reasonable modern estimates suggest perhaps 100,000 trials between 1450 and 1750, with something between 40,000 and 50,000 executions, of which 20 to 25 percent were men.... these figures are chilling enough, but they have to be set in the context of what was probably the harshest period of **capital punishment** in European history."

[www.genocide.org]

The website further states:

"Indeed, it is arguable that at no other time in European history have adult women been targeted *selectively*, on such a scale, for torture and annihilation."

In massacring so many people through fear and ignorance, Christianity must take responsibility for stunting the natural psychic development of the human race. In fact it should be noted that the lands or property of those convicted of witchcraft were seized and the family had to pay costs for the trial. All this money went to the Church, so you could say that in essence, the wealth of the Churches of the day was built upon blood money.

William Tyndale (c.1492-1536)

English Protestant and Humanist, found guilty of heresy. He was strangled at the stake and his body burnt. So what was his crime? He merely wanted to bring the Bible to the ordinary people at a time when only the scholars/clergy had access to it, for they were the only ones with an ability to read the Latin and Greek translations.

He was forced to leave England in 1524 because the church considered him a threat to their monopoly as the translators and 'true' guardians of the scriptures. In 1525 the New Testament was published and was smuggled from Germany to England. An outraged Henry VIII accused Tyndale of spreading sedition and all his work was banned in England, although he did still publish parts of the Old Testament in Holland. Unfortunately when he travelled to Antwerp, Belgium in 1535 he was arrested, accused of heresy and consequently found guilty. Despite all this, history shows Tyndale's Bible translations were taken and incorporated into what is known today as the King James Bible.

Galileo (1564-1642)

Aristotle believed that the Earth was stationary and the centre of the universe, contrary to Copernicus' belief that the Earth revolved around the Sun which upset the religious leaders who considered it to be the work of the Devil. Galileo supported Copernicus' findings and as a result found himself facing the Inquisition.

The website www.galileo.rice.edu informs the enquirer that in 1633 a transcript was found forbidding Galileo to discuss, orally or in writing, the theory that the sun was the centre of the universe, since this was considered absurd in theologian philosophy and thus heretical in nature. In 1624 Pope Urban VIII assured Galileo that he could continue his work provided it was based solely upon mathematical theory. However, later in June 1633 the Pope decided Galileo should be imprisoned, there was a formal threat of torture, and religious penances.

William Shakespeare (1564-1616)

Shakespeare lived during the era when the witch hunts were at their height across Europe (1550-1650) and yet throughout our research, although largely restricted to the internet, we found no record that 'Hamlet' was banned or even caused controversy to this effect. This seems strange considering that the lead character, Hamlet, conversed openly with a 'Spirit', despite the fact that such an act would, at the time, have been interpreted as conversing with a 'demon' and as such would have resulted in a trial.

As men had no immunity from execution for witchcraft and as the plays were performed live, it seems inconceivable that such a performance, in front of a large crowd, would not have caused mass hysteria. Yet as stated, there is no record of any such outcry or condemnation, even though the religious leaders of the day would have known of the play's contents, albeit after the event. Also Shakespeare wrote about the witches in 'Macbeth', which was even more blatant in its content and yet even though it was written at the height of religious literalism/ fundamentalism, it too received no recorded criticism of any kind.

Shakespeare's character Hamlet would have had to have been clairvoyant and clairaudient to see and hear Spirit, as well as Dickens' character Scrooge. So do orthodox Christians condemn these classic works of literature as the mouthpiece of the Devil? If they do, it is sad. If they do not, why the exception?

Emanuel Swedenborg (1688-1772)

Swedish philosopher, scientist, mystic, prophet and visionary. He was not a dreamer as often portrayed, but a practical scientist who preferred the real business of mining than becoming a Professor of Astronomy. Swedenborg was aware of the scepticism and criticism of his beliefs and he wrote the following in his first theological work:

"I am well aware that many persons will insist that

75

it is impossible for anyone to converse with Spirits and with angels during his life time in the body; many will say that such intercourse must be mere fancy; some, that I have invented such relations in order to gain credit; whilst others will make objections. For all these, however, I care not, since I have seen, heard and felt."

[The Occult and the Supernatural]

Others noted certain aspects of his beliefs:

"Swedenborg spoke as if heaven and its inhabitants were his 'second home'. He knows them as he knows human beings and his knowledge enables him to maintain that man's real self is in form exactly as is his physical body, and if it had not been for the Fall, the body would have been sloughed off like a snake-skin. Instead, it is quite essential for men to die before they move on to a higher place."

[The Occult and the Supernatural]

The emphasis is on being human, and seeing and understanding God in human terms and perceptions. After his death, The Swedenborgian Church or New Church as it was known, was founded, and even today Swedenborgism is very popular and still practiced in Sweden.

At the time of the French Revolution, Britain had a free press and Swedenborg's writings were published in Britain instead of Sweden. However, Britain soon banned the formation of new societies resulting in Thomas Paine fleeing to Paris after his book 'The Rights of Man' was published.
[www.swedenborg.org.uk quoting from 'Blake the artist and Swedenborg' by Patrick L. Johnson]

Incidentally, Daniel Eton was sentenced to 18 months imprisonment plus a spell in the pillory each month for publishing Thomas Paine's book, 'The Age of Reason', that criticised the Christian faith.

Witchcraft Act 1735
Introduced as a means to prosecute anyone claiming to act as a Spiritualistic Medium or believed to be exercising any powers of telepathy, clairvoyance or other similar powers, or in doing so to use fraudulent devices. Although not repealed in its entirety until the introduction of the Fraudulent Mediums Act, 1951, much of the relevant implications of the Act were incorporated within section 4 of the Vagrancy Act, 1824.

William Blake (1757-1827)
English poet, artist and visionary, illustrated the Bible, works by Dante and Shakespeare, as well as his own work. His illustrations and poems were often inspired by visions/Spirit. Blake openly stated that he took great comfort and inspiration from communication with his 'deceased' brother. In 1789 Blake joined the Swedenborgian New Church.

Blake is recognised today as one of the giants of the 'romantic period', but like many of the famous painters, fame and popularity was posthumous. Poverty did not worry him for Blake did not value materialism; an integral part of Spiritualist beliefs. The website www.ipoet.com states the following about Blake:

> "A self-educated, free thinking rebel and Spiritualist, Blake reportedly found his poetic and artistic inspiration via periodic encounters with angels and other heavenly Spirits. When he was but ten years old Blake observed a 'host of angels sitting in a tree.' When he was twenty, he saw his dying brother's soul 'ascend heavenward clapping its hands for

joy.'.....Blake was ahead of his time and never achieved significant financial success or popular appreciation until after his death."

Blake believed he was under the direction of 'messengers from Heaven' and in his picture 'The Spirit of Fountain Court' he clearly depicts his bedroom as having Spirit visitors. In reference to his prophetic poem 'Milton', Blake commented:

> "I have written this poem from immediate dictation, twelve or sometimes twenty or thirty lines at a time, without premeditation, and even against my will."
>
> [The Unexplained, by Fraser Stewart]

William Henry Harrison (1773-1841)

At the time of going to press we were unable to obtain a copy of 'The haunting of the Presidents' by Joel Martin and William J. Birnes, therefore the following has been taken from the website www.victorzammit.com:

> True story - American President Harrison was governor of Indiana Territory and in 1811 led the slaughter of the Shawnee Red Indians and took their lands. The Red Indian Psychic/Medicine Man, Tenskwatawa, predicted that Harrison would be killed in office when he became President. Years later in 1840, when Harrison became President, he lasted just 4 weeks in office – then he mysteriously died. All were stunned because it was the first time a President had died in office. Tenskwatawa also predicted that an American President elected in a year ending in a zero, would die in office.

Below is a list that clearly vindicates his prediction;

1840 - President Harrison elected and died in office.
1860 - Abraham Lincoln killed in office.
1880 - President Garfield was also killed in office.
1900 - President W. McKinley elected and killed in office.
1920 - President W. G. Harding elected and died in office.
1940 - President Franklin D. Roosevelt elected for a third term, died in office.
1960 - President Kennedy elected and killed in office.
1980 - President Ronald Reagan elected and survived an assassin's bullet. It is believed his wife Nancy sought psychic protection against the Presidential curse.
2000 - President George W. Bush elected and...?

Allan Kardec (1804-1869)

The mediumship of Hippolyte Léon Denizard Rivail has a great influence in Brazil where Spirit temples have been erected. Rivail, using the pseudonym of Allan Kardec, compiled the book; 'The Spirits' Book'. The book comprises of questions and answers attributed to Spirit whilst Kardec was in a trance state. A footnote in the book informs the reader that 'Rivail is buried in Paris' famous Pére-Lachaise cemetery, where his tomb annually draws more visitors than any other.' That was one popular Spiritualist Medium!

Abraham Lincoln (1809-1865)

Spiritualists were often guests at the White House, but today's Lincoln scholars are split as to whether Lincoln actually attended séances. From a Spiritualist perspective; if you are a regular guest there will be some form or another of 'séance'. The website www.prairieghosts.com reports that during a séance held by Nettie Maynard in 1863 a grand piano levitated:

> "The medium was playing the instrument when it began to rise off the floor. Lincoln and Colonel Simon Kase were both present and it was said that both men climbed onto the piano, only to have it jump and shake so hard that they climbed down. It is recorded that Lincoln would later refer to the levitation as proof of an 'invisible power'."

It is also alleged that Lincoln asked Dr Bamford, a Spirit communicator, for advice in respect of the Federal Army on the front lines. Lincoln acted on the advice given, and along with his wife Mary visited the battle front, listened to the troops grievances, and rallied them together. Many attribute the advice from Spirit as the beginning of the turning point of the war.

Many perceive Lincoln as a Christian President, but Lincoln did not believe Jesus was the Christ of God as understood by the Christian church. In public Lincoln avoided Spiritualists but privately they were welcomed, and certainly his wife Mary embraced Spiritualists openly. Lincoln himself dreamt that he would be assassinated a few days before that fatal night in the Ford Theatre. The precognitive dream was related to his close friend, Ward Hill Lamon:

> "About ten days ago, I retired very late. I soon began to dream. There seemed to be a death-like stillness about me. Then I heard subdued sobs, as if a number of people were weeping. I thought I left my bed and wandered downstairs. There the silence was broken by the same pitiful sobbing, but the mourners were invisible. I went from room to room. No living

person was in sight, but the same mournful sounds met me as I passed alone. I was puzzled and alarmed. Determined to find the cause of a state of things so mysterious and shocking, I kept on until I arrived at the East room. Before me was a catafalque on which rested a corpse wrapped in funeral vestments. Around it were stationed soldiers who were acting as guards; and there was a throng of people, some gazing mournfully upon the corpse, whose face was covered, others weeping pitifully. 'Who is dead in the White house?' I demanded of one of the soldiers. 'The president,' was his answer. 'He was killed by an assassin'."

[www.paranormal.about.com]

Charles Dickens (1812-1870)

In one of Dickens' best loved novels, 'A Christmas Carol', he brings the Spirit of Scrooge's ex-partner Joseph Marley as well as the Spirits of past, present and future, to help convince Scrooge to change his miserable ways, in effect to create a better karma; you reap what you sow. Maybe Dickens was inspired by Shakespeare; Macbeth's Banquo and Hamlet's father bringing warnings from 'beyond the grave'. On the subject of inspiration, Fraser Stewart states in his book 'The Unexplained':

> "Charles Dickens relates that as he dozed in his chair, characters would enter his imagination, as it were, begging to be set down on paper."

George Eliot - pen name of Mary Ann Evans (1819-1880)

She was under no illusion as to where the greatest influence upon her work came from and made no secret of the fact:

> "...that when she was producing her best work,

some Spirit, who was 'not herself' took over from
her normal personality."
[The Unexplained, Fraser Stewart]

Emily Brontë (1818-1848)
It is said that Emily Brontë would enter into an ecstatic trance
state but she considered them to be very mundane. This raises
the question; how valuable were they in terms of inspiration for
her characters and poems?

Queen Victoria (1819-1901)
It was generally acknowledged that Queen Victoria used the
services of Trance Medium, John Brown. She also admired and
sought out the Medium, Robert James Lees, who at the age of 19
was already giving demonstrations of clairvoyance.

Vagrancy Act 1824
Introduced as a means of controlling the activities of the
increasing influx of travellers to the streets of England and Wales.
Most of the Act dealt in general with the actions of those classed
as rogues and vagabonds, but section 4 specifically dealt with
any means of obtaining monies through mediumship, e.g.
palmistry, fortune telling, etc. Used in conjunction with the
Witchcraft Act, Section 4 remained in effect until its substitution
by the Fraudulent Mediums Act, 1951.

The birth of Modern Spiritualism 1848
In Hydesville, New York, USA, two sisters by the name of
Margaretta and Catherine Fox, responded to rappings that were
occurring in their home. They managed to establish a
communication link with the Spirit by using one rap for 'yes'
and two raps for 'no'. The Spirit communicator was a peddler
who had been killed by the previous occupants and was buried
in the cellar. Margaretta and Catherine both confessed to the

rappings having been a fraud, but then retracted the statement saying the confessions were a result of financial difficulty.

In 1849 the first Spiritualist meeting was held, with their sister Leah, who became the first professional modern Medium. The sisters attracted a lot of attention, home circles became very popular and Spiritualist societies were created in America.

Spiritualism was brought to the UK in 1852 by Mrs Hayden who as a result was slated by the press and the religious men of the time. However, this did not curb the popularity of Spiritualism developing and expanding in the UK.

Leonora Piper (1857-1950)

An American Medium, she was investigated by the Australian lawyer, Richard Hodgson who, due to his unrelenting determination in exposing fraudulent Psychics, was employed by the Society for Psychical Research (SPR). Hodgson even hired private detectives to try and prove that Leonora Piper was obtaining knowledge of her sitters prior to their readings, as well as planting people during her demonstrations in order to trick her. Despite all his efforts, Hodgson never proved that she was a fraudulent Medium.

One of Leonora's Spirit controls was George Pellow, who just happened to have been a good friend of Hodgson when he was 'alive'. This gave Hodgson the opportunity to question Pellow and introduce family and friends. The outcome of that was Hodgson became a convert to Spiritualism! The irony is; Hodgson died unexpectedly, and soon after his 'death' wasted no time in becoming a Spirit control of Leonora Piper!

Sir Arthur Conan Doyle (1859-1930)

Best known as the creator of the logical thinking detective Sherlock Holmes. In later life Doyle became a Spiritualist and enthusiastically promoted Spiritualism through public talks. He was well known as a supporter of the research and work into

Spirit activities carried out by Sir William Crookes and as such penned the appendix to the scientist's book, 'Researches in the phenomena of Spiritualism', published in 1926.

William Butler (W.B.) Yeats (1865-1939)

Irish poet, dramatist and Nobel prize winner for literature, married the Medium Georgie Hyde-Lees, who helped Yeats to re-enforce his Spiritualist beliefs. Yeats admired Blake's 'Spiritualism' and was probably introduced to Swedenborg while editing Blake's 'Prophetic Books' in 1893. He read a lot about Swedenborg and as a result he wanted to bring change in the way the public perceived Spiritualism. He achieved this through his work on psychical research, which included lecturing on psychic phenomena.

Sir Winston Churchill (1874-1965)

In November 2002, the BBC created a television programme to find 'the greatest Briton of all time', and following a nationwide poll, Sir Winston Churchill was voted the clear winner. But few would have been aware that the Medium, Bertha Harris visited Sir Winston Churchill and Lady Churchill on a regular basis, or that Bertha correctly predicted, six months before the events of Pearl Harbour, that the U.S. would join the war. Even General de Gaulle regularly visited Bertha Harris and used her mediumistic skills effectively.

The official website of Helen Duncan states:

> "Churchill was no stranger to psychic phenomena. Recalling the events of the Boer War when he had been captured, had escaped and seeking sanctuary he explained in his autobiography how he was 'guided by some form of mental planchette (a Spiritualist tool) to the only house in a 30 mile radius that was sympathetic to the British cause'. Had he knocked on the back door of any other house he

would have been arrested and returned to the Boer commanders to be shot as an escaping prisoner of war. Many years prior to this he had been inducted into the Grand Ancient Order of Druids. And throughout his life he experienced many times when his psychic sense saved his life."

[www.members.tripod.com]

The website www.paranormal.about.com relates the following article submitted by Mark McCarthy concerning Churchill and Lincoln:

"During one of Winston Churchill's visits to the United States during WW2, he spent the night in the White House. Churchill loved to retire late, take a long, hot bath while drinking a Scotch, and smoke a cigar and relax. On this occasion, he climbed out of the bath and naked, but for his cigar, walked into the adjoining bedroom. He was startled to see Abraham Lincoln standing by the fireplace in the room, leaning on the mantle. Churchill, always quick on the uptake, blinked and said 'Good evening, Mr. President. You seem to have me at a disadvantage.' Lincoln smiled softly and disappeared."

The Society for Psychical Research (SPR) 1882
The society's aim was to examine telepathy, hypnotism, apparitions and physical phenomena within Spiritualism in a scientific and unprejudiced approach. Among the original founders were F.W.H. Myers, Sir William Barrett and Edmund Gurney. The SPR is still in existence today in America and London.

Two Worlds 1887
This magazine, which is still popular today, was founded by the

Medium, Emma Hardinge-Britten who edited it herself for the first five years of its publication.

The Spiritualist National Union (SNU) 1890

An organisation also set up by Emma Hardinge-Britten, in the hope of uniting the many different Spiritualist churches. Through trance mediumship, her Spirit Communicator, Robert Owen, gave the seven principles on which the SNU is based.

Helen Duncan (1897-1956)

Practising Spiritualists in the UK today owe a great debt of gratitude to Helen Duncan, because the turning point for Modern Spiritualism came with the events that the Materialisation Medium put in motion. In fact for instigating those events she was to pay dearly; with her life.

As a means of explanation: A Materialisation Medium or Physical Medium is used by Spirit, while in the trance state, to produce from their body a substance known as ectoplasm. Spirit are then able to 'mould' the ectoplasm so as to materialise into a virtual physical form, as they would have looked during their previous lifetime. Such a form would be solid to the touch, and able to walk and talk. This form of physical phenomena was very rare, yet it is well documented that during World War II, those servicemen that lost their lives would materialise through Helen Duncan.

> "When she (Helen Duncan) materialised the full form of a sailor with the name HMS Barham on his cap, a ship, which the English government denied had been sunk; she was arrested and jailed as a spy and then a witch. Even after she was proved correct, she was held as a witch…"
>
> [The Helen Duncan official website: www.members.tripod.com]

Subsequently Helen Duncan was sentenced to nine months imprisonment at Holloway Gaol and was also denied the right of appeal to the House of Lords. Helen Duncan's official website reports that;

> "It was not only the best legal minds in the country that felt this case had been a major miscarriage of justice. So too did her prison warders."
>
> ...During her 9 months, Helen Duncan's cell door was never locked, and she continued to link with Spirit for her fellow inmates and warders, and visitors "...including Britain's Prime Minister Sir Winston Churchill..."
>
> [www.members.tripod.com]

It must be noted that after her release, through a combination of the effects of her imprisonment and the increase in demand for séances, the quality of Helen Duncan's mediumship suffered. In 1956, a Police raid during a materialisation resulted in her death after the rush of ectoplasm back into her body caused two second degree burns to the stomach. She was taken to hospital and five weeks later returned back to the Spirit World. Incidentally, during the raid the Police strip-searched Helen Duncan and found no evidence of a fraudulent nature.

Queen Elizabeth, The Queen Mother (1900-2002)
On the website www.victorzammit.com it states that;

> "the Queen Mother often used the services of the Medium Lillian Bailey to communicate with her late husband, King George VI."

Michael Bentine (1922-1996)

A highly respected and much loved member of the 'Goons' comedy quartet. While on active duty during WWII, he would clairvoyantly 'see' the 'face of death' on those young men who were destined not to return. He even saw the face super-imposed over that of his own son, but having ignored his father's warning, the son fulfilled the prediction by failing to return.

The Greater World Christian Spiritualist League 1931

Founded through the trance mediumship of wheelchair-bound, Winifred Moyes and her Spirit Guide, Zodiac. Zodiac claimed to be one of the teachers of the law in the Temple of Jerusalem referred to in Mark 12:28-34. Their beliefs are very much based upon a combination of traditional Christian ideology and communication with the Spirit World. Today the organisation is better known as the Greater World Christian Spiritualist Association (GWCSA).

Psychic News 1932

Founded by Maurice Barbanell, the Medium for the UK Spiritualist Movement's best loved Spirit Guide, Silver Birch. The newspaper, which is still popular today, acts primarily as the informative and philosophical arm of the SNU.

Fraudulent Mediums Act 1951

Introduced to repeal the Witchcraft Act, 1735, that had been used to prosecute Physical Medium, Helen Duncan and also the relevant provisions of section 4 of the Vagrancy Act, 1824. Following the trial and subsequent treatment of Helen Duncan, whom he was known to have visited during her incarceration, it is believed that Sir Winston Churchill exerted influence to have the law changed in favour of allowing genuine Mediums to practice without fear of prosecution.

Legal recognition 1954

More than a century on from the initial rappings heard by the Fox sisters, Spiritualism gained official recognition from the Government as a bona fide religion in the UK. This allowed Spiritualists to practice openly without fear of prosecution. However it was not until the introduction of the Human Rights Act, 1998, that all barriers concerning equality in the acceptance of religious practices were finally removed. Good examples of this were the introduction of TV programmes relating to Spiritualist Mediums in communication with the 'deceased' loved ones of studio audiences, and more recently the entertainment programmes 'Afterlife' and 'Medium'.

Religious trends 2000

In the 2000 census taken in Brazil; 1.3% of the population (2,262,401) are followers of Allan Kardec (Spiritist), known as 'Kardecists'. In contrast 74% identify themselves as Roman Catholics and yet children were being shot on the streets of Brazil. Where is the spirituality of their faith? Why is there not a public outcry because of this situation by their religious representatives/ leaders in the Vatican? Why does the Vatican not invest some of its wealth not only to redress this situation but also the poverty of Catholic communities worldwide?

Modern Spirtualism 2005

The knowledge and acceptance of 'Spirit', through apparitions and Mediums, is reflected in our world history and has influenced civilisations on a religious/spirituality basis for many centuries. Even though civilisations have become more 'civilised' as well as scientifically and technologically advanced, people are still relating stories of seeing 'ghosts', the Spirits of loved ones recently passed, etc. If this was a fad, why has it remained so prevalent in so many societies in one form or another?

Forms of Spiritualism are recorded as the 2nd biggest in Brazil and 1st in Sweden. Shamanism is still practiced by the Native American Indians and there are Spiritualist centres, churches and organisations all around the world. Even the TV programme, 'Miracles of Roma Downey', often relates stories of people who have been saved by their 'Guardian Angels'. Why do people talk to the photographs and at the gravestone's of loved ones? What is the point if there is no hope of being heard? For many believe that their departed loved ones are still around, listening and protecting them; acting as their Guardian Angels, which in effect are Spirit that may or may not be known to them.

PHILOSOPHY
OF
SPIRITUALISM

Philosophy

Anti-Spiritualists condemn Spiritualism as the bringer of spiritual darkness to the world, the work of devil co-operation, but we, to date, have never read any of these slatings referring to our spiritual philosophy on life and the afterlife. If you the reader are an anti-Spiritualist; do you know what our philosophy on life actually is? Do you know that you can tell a lot about a person by their attitude and outlook on life? We ask you; does Spiritualist philosophy confirm the Christian faith's accusation that we are working for the Devil?

Philosophy should be used as a tool to help us on the pathway of spiritual progression, by seeking knowledge that inspires us to think, study and even criticise our current beliefs to ensure they do not stagnate over time, that the beliefs are always progressive, changing with the times as our knowledge and understanding develops. To us, philosophy represents the freedom of thought, the weapon against religious doctrines that are inflexible and at times unreasonable.

We agree with Thomas Paine's sentiment in the dedication he made in his book 'The Age of Reason', in fact we at ETVOS have made it our philosophical motto:

> "....I have always strenuously supported the Right of every man to his opinion, however different that opinion might be to mine. He who denies to another this right, makes a slave of himself to his present opinion, because he precludes himself the right of changing it.
>
> The most formidable weapon against errors of every kind is Reason. I have never used any other, and I trust I never shall."

It is a shame that many religious leaders do not follow Thomas Paine's example.

God

The Spiritualist's God advocates equal rights, does not care what religious beliefs you have, if any, and is only concerned that you are a good, caring person. We are monotheist like many mainstream religions, for we are taught that the ancestral worship of 'many gods', such as those worshipped by the ancient Greeks and in the Roman empire, is wrong. These cultures had a god for everything. They covered every aspect of their life with a supernatural/omnipotent being. Ironically we have not left the past behind in religious terms, we have merely reversed the situation; rather than one belief – many gods, it is now one God – many beliefs. Spiritually we wish to believe that we are more civilized by worshiping just the one God, but in essence we are no different from our forefathers.

Modern society's monotheistic God is divided into many 'images' and the belief system into many branches. For instance, within Christian-based religions alone there are Catholics, Baptists, Jehovah's Witnesses, to name but a few, and they all believe that 'their' God is the 'true' God. This same belief extends to all the monotheistic religions worldwide. What they fail to see, what their elitist views have blinkered them to, is that in reality we are all worshipping many 'images' of the same God, the only difference being the name used. A good example of this can be seen in the numerous interpretations of the image of the Buddha that can be seen worldwide. The shockingly harsh reality for the majority of religions is that there is only <u>one</u> God, one who is not concerned with religious elitism, doctrines, rituals, etc., but only you the individual.

Virgin birth

Spiritualists believe that Jesus was in fact as restricted by his human form as indeed we all are and that there was no miraculous birth, no immaculate conception, for to have been so would have been a physical violation; a woman instructed that she was going to give birth to a son, irrespective if she wanted to or not.

If a young woman – your daughter – said to you, "An Angel of God told me I would give birth to a boy," and insisted that she was still a virgin, what would you believe? Your daughter? Would you be concerned that your daughter was caught up in some religious cult and had been taken advantage of, as well as being convinced into believing she was having God's child?

In the whole scenario there is no option, no choice, no freewill. What would have been the outcome if the young woman had refused to accept the pregnancy; having no wish to start a family? Does this not bear all the hallmarks of a Zeus-type god; a selfish dictator? If you cannot accept the virgin birth how can you accept the books of Leviticus and Deuteronomy that are used to condemn the practices of Spiritualism?

Silver cord

The general belief in the Spiritualist Movement is that the lifeforce is connected to the physical body via a silver cord; a kind of spiritual umbilical cord, and upon the death of the physical body the silver cord detaches itself and the spirit returns to the Spirit World.

However, we believe that although the concept of a silver cord is acceptable in the understanding that there is in fact a link, the reality is that it is only symbolic. What can be 'seen' by clairvoyants is the vibrational link of the lifeforce anchored to the physical body.

The Bible refers to the subject in Ecclesiastes 12:5-7, saying;

> [5]....and desire no longer is stirred. Then people go to their eternal home and mourners go about the streets.

> [6]Remember him-before the silver cord is severed or

the golden bowl is broken; before the pitcher is shattered at the spring, or the wheel broken at the well, [7]and the dust returns to the ground it came from, and the spirit returns to God who gave it.

As Spiritualists we would interpret this as meaning:

- Towards the end of your life you do not crave things of your youth. Age and wisdom has replaced desire.
- Upon the death of the physical body your Spirit returns to the Spirit World; Man's real home and those you leave behind grieve for you.
- Value the person while they are alive, do not leave it too late.
- The silver cord detaches itself, whereupon the physical body, being of organic matter, decomposes and returns to the earth ('dust to dust'), while the Spirit continues back to the Spirit World.
- This is the will of God. God allowed Spirit to express itself through organic matter in order to evolve spiritually, so that we may return a little closer to spiritual perfection; God.

Jesus

Jesus was a philosopher, Healer and Medium. He taught an alternative perception of God and how we should interact with each other. Jesus saw the needy, the poor and recognised them as a valid part of society, and helped them the best way he could. He inspired thousands at the time, supporting his claims through acts of healing, mediumship and spiritual guidance. Jesus was neither a redeemer nor a part of the trinity as portrayed later by the Christian Church.

We perceive this redemption as an easy way out from not taking responsibility for your actions during your life. Feeling sorry for yourself and seeking forgiveness through the Church before you 'die', just in case the religious folk are right, is not going to save you. You cannot hide from your actions.

The Bible says Jesus died for our sins and we can obtain salvation in his name, thus Jesus has been perceived as the redeemer, but we challenge this perception. Jesus did not teach 'redemption' that will lead to salvation, he taught personal responsibility:

- Jesus always maintained his beliefs, he never denied them and was prepared to pay the consequences for his actions.
- Jesus knew he would be betrayed, but he did not flee.
- Peter did not take responsibility and denied knowing Jesus three times.
- Judas, upon realising what he had done, took responsibility for his actions by the only way he knew; the taking of his own life.

The Crucifixion and Personal Responsibility

Christians believe Jesus suffered on the cross and sacrificed himself so that the collective sins of humanity could be forgiven. This ideology raises two points;

> 1. Why would an all-loving Father (God) send his Son to suffer and die a horrific death for the sake of others? Shouldn't humanity have taken responsibility for their actions rather than have had a 'scapegoat' to wipe the slate clean? What lesson can be learnt by the wrongdoer if their sins; past, present and future, can be erased through penance in church? How do they learn compassion if not by experience? After all, the Bible tells us that God made Adam and Eve take responsibility for their actions, so why not humanity? Has God 'moved the goalposts'?

2. Jesus is believed to be the <u>only</u> Son of God and that as part of the trinity he is the manifestation of God. Therefore, if God is an omnipotent being and expressed himself through Jesus Christ, did Jesus really suffer on the cross since God would not have felt any pain? Why should Jesus have had any doubts as expressed when he reportedly cried out, 'My God, my God, why have you forsaken me?'

Reap what you sow
An adage that was emphasised by Jesus in his teachings to the disciples, the primary element being one of personal responsibility for one's own actions and the consequences of them. In effect it was a study of what some religions refer to as 'karma'.

The majority of religions instil a somewhat false philosophy of great reward for those that serve faithfully coupled with the fear of punishment for those who do not. In comparison, Spiritualism has a more liberal, positive outlook; we do not lose our family and friends to 'death', and there is neither hell for bad actions nor a select few that are chosen to sit at God's side. If you choose to do bad acts in your life, you must be prepared to accept responsibility for those actions and make amends accordingly.

A good example of this is shown with regards to forgiveness: Over time you will need to seek the forgiveness of those you have wronged. Failure in gaining that forgiveness will restrict your spiritual progression, but in keeping with the natural balance of the Universal Laws, those that cannot forgive will in turn be restricted. It may be that you end up spending literally centuries seeking the forgiveness of one particular Spirit being that you hurt during your physical life. Imagine that scenario in the case of the likes of Hitler, Stalin, 'Papa Doc' Duvalier of the Republic of Haiti, to name but a few.

PHILOSOPHY FROM SPIRIT GUIDES

As mentioned previously, Spiritualism comprises of the Greek Philosophers' ethics and the religious concerns for an individual's destiny after 'death'. Spiritualism does not have a 'Holy Book' to follow or gain inspiration from. We draw our philosophy from two main sources:

1. Spirit
2. Spiritualist Mediums

1. SPIRIT

We felt it was important to quote a few philosophical extracts from some of the Spiritualist Movement's most prominent and best loved Spirit Guides, given through the trance state. So if you are an anti-Spiritualist and of the view that we are devil worshippers, then please explain how this is reflected in the following Spirit philosophy:

White Eagle, Spirit Guide of Grace Cooke
In 'Prayer in the New Age' (pg 78), White Eagle speaks to the people who came to listen to a service in the Lodge;

> "...You enter to worship, to forget for a brief space of physical life, and feel your oneness with God; and to give service. You have come to serve, we in Spirit have also come to serve all men on their path to the Father/Mother God."

and White Eagle on the subject of spiritual service, from 'Spiritual Unfoldment 3' (pg 50);

> "So, beloved children, we would leave you with this thought. Daily endeavour to guide good thought, kind

thought into the world. It is so simple. The life of the true Christ man is a positive force which can affect all of mankind. In the degree that you give out good thought you attract to yourself forces of good, you reach to the light and the Spiritual life, and so you are building the golden temple of the soul."

Red Cloud, Spirit Guide of Estelle Roberts

In 'Red Cloud Speaks' (pg 75), on the subject of 'Where is Spiritualism leading you?' Red Cloud comments;

"Is it [Spiritualism] going to lead you through the spheres [many mansions], or is it going to take you down to hell? I am going to answer that question very frankly. You have free will. You have personal responsibility. If you want to go to the lower states of existence, you will go. Neither I nor any dogma or creed can put you there."

In the 1930's the colour of a man's skin was an issue, for racism was rife and a question asked of Red Cloud was; Was the white man better than the black man? Red Cloud's response was;

"...The Law operates upon one and all. The colour of your skin or eyes or anything in your material does not matter. It is the soul-body, and how you use it, that counts most. Remember Jesus of Nazareth was not a white man, yet if only white men could emulate what Jesus of Nazareth did of his own free will!"

In Sept. 1936 Red Cloud also said,

"Remember, to know God is to love your fellow

men; to worship God is to serve them; to believe in
God is to succour them; and to see God is to bring
peace amongst the nations."

Silver Birch, Spirit Guide of Maurice Barbanell

Probably the best known and loved Spirit Guide within the
Spiritualist Movement. In 'Lift up your Hearts', Silver Birch
expressed the following;

> "...Remember always that primarily you are
> Spiritual beings expressing yourselves through
> physical bodies. You are not bodies with Spirits,
> you are Spirits with bodies. Strive always so to order
> your lives that your Spiritual nature will rise to the
> heights. And may the power of the Great White
> Spirit bless you all."

And Silver Birch, on the subject of personal responsibility; the
philosophy of 'you reap what you sow';

> "There is no cheating. The Law will always operate
> – Physically you can pretend, Spiritually you
> cannot. Physically you are a closed book,
> Spiritually you are an open page. This is the great
> difference.
>
> Progress is achieved because you have earned
> it. There are no instant methods of achieving
> Spiritual mastery. Every step must be taken
> successively. You become what you have made
> yourself to be by the way you live. No one can
> deflect or change in any way that immutable
> sequence of cause and effect in your lives.
>
> That is how the Law works. Thus does the Great
> Spirit ensure that justice always will be done, not

necessarily in your world of matter, but it will operate when you come to our side of life."

Allan Kardec

From the vast amount of data obtained through the mediumship of Allan Kardec, we have selected a few questions along with the relative responses, that we believe will be of interest:

> Q. How can we ascertain whether a suggested thought comes from a good Spirit or from an evil one?
> A. "Study its quality – good Spirits give only good counsels. It is for you to distinguish between the good and the bad." (pg 226)

> Q. What is to be understood by the expression, 'Guardian-angel'?
> A. "A Spirit protector of high degree." (pg 490)

Nowadays the answer would refer to Spirit Guides, for the term 'Guardian Angel' is interchangeable to incorporate any Spirit that offers assistance, such as Helpers, loved ones, etc.

> Q. What is the mission of a Spirit protector?
> A. "That of a father towards his children – to lead the object of his protection into the right road, to aid him with his counsels, to console him in his afflictions, and to sustain his courage under the trials of his earthly life." (pg 491)

It should be noted that the Spirit protector/helper may not be able to protect the individual if they allow a negative Spirit to influence them. You have free will to accept good or bad counsel.

Ramadahn, Spirit Guide of Ursula Roberts

In 'Wisdom of Ramadan' (pg 97), the Spirit Guide is questioned about the number of religious beliefs and philosophies there are, to which he replies:

> Q. "There are many beliefs and philosophies, yet all think their way is best?"
>
> A. "When you come to the end of your earthly experience and step forth from the physical body into the new life it will not be asked of you: 'What religion did you follow? What belief did you hold?' There will be none to say: 'Were you a Roman Catholic, a Hindu, a Jew or a Christian?' But those who have loved you in your earth life, these will come to you with love. They will look to see how much service you have rendered, how much love you have given to those weaker and less evolved than yourself, how much courage you have shown in dark and lonely experiences, for by this measure is the soul known when it comes to the spirit life.
>
> But where spiritual knowledge has given the soul increased ability to live kindly and peacefully, then we say that religious belief has its value. Where a philosophy helps to raise the thoughts on high, then that philosophy is a true one. But it is not true that worship in any one church or belief or any one religion is more important than the other"

2. SPIRITUALIST MEDIUMS

An important part of the 'religious' service of Spiritualism is the philosophy. This entails the Medium giving a talk, referred to as an 'address', for an average of 20 minutes duration. This philosophy can take the form of;

- Inspirational speaking - from Spirit or inspired by a reading given by a church service attendee
- An inspired piece of written work from the Medium
- A relevant personal experience
- A particular point/topic - i.e. materialism, selfishness, courage, etc.

It does not matter if the philosophy derives from Spirit or the Medium, it generally makes reference to;
- Service to others
- Respect to everyone and everything
- A good turn done (rather than a bad one)
- Reaping what you sow - taking responsibility for your actions
- Strength in adversity - overcoming a difficult situation in life
- Kindness and compassion
- Forgiveness
- Judgement/perception - a tramp may be more spiritually evolved than the most prominent religious leaders

Basic messages include;
- You are Spirit expressing itself through organic matter
- You have selected to come here for a reason, to learn a particular life lesson
- Reincarnation - the possible need to incarnate again to learn a particular lesson you failed to learn previously for whatever reason.

SPIRITUALIST ORGANISATIONS

The following are four of the most prominent Spiritualist organisations in the UK and offer good examples of the way beliefs are structured within the Spiritualist Movement:

Spiritualist National Union (SNU)

Based on an individual's interpretation of the following seven principles:

- The Fatherhood of God
- The Brotherhood of Man
- The Communion of Spirits and the Ministry of Angels
- The continuous existence of the human soul
- Personal responsibility
- Compensation and retribution hereafter for all the good and evil deeds done on earth
- Eternal progress open to every human soul

The Greater World (Christian Spiritualist Association)

Founded in 1931 as The Greater World Christian Spiritualist League.

Beliefs:

- I believe in one God who is Love.
- I accept the Leadership of Jesus the Christ.
- I believe that God manifests through the illimitable power of holy spirit.
- I believe in the survival of the soul and its individuality after physical death.
- I believe in Communion with God, with His angelic ministers, and with souls functioning in conditions other than Earth Life.
- I believe that all forms of Life created by God intermingle, are interdependent, and evolve until perfection is attained.
- I believe in perfect justice of the Divine Laws governing all Life.
- I believe that sins committed can only be rectified by the sinner himself or herself, through the redemptive power of Jesus the Christ, by repentance and service to others.

The Pledge:
* I will at all times endeavour to be guided in my thoughts, words, and deeds by the teaching and example of Jesus the Christ.

The Spiritualist Association of Great Britain (SAGB)
Based on the following seven principles:
* We believe in an Infinite Intelligence, which governs all.
* We believe that personal identity and all sentient forms of life survive physical death.
* We believe that continuous existence and eternal progress occur for all in the Hereafter.
* We believe in communion with spiritual realms.
* We believe that all humanity is spiritually linked.
* We believe that in the Hereafter, all must account for their actions on earth and will judge themselves accordingly.
* We believe that all are responsible for the way they conduct their earthly lives.

Philosophy and purpose:
The primary purpose of the Association is to offer evidence, through mediumship, of the continuation of the personality after physical death and to relieve suffering through spiritual healing.

United Spiritualists
Aims:
* Unification of all people having a spiritualist belief and furtherance of the spiritualist cause.
* The promotion of quality healing, mediumship, philosophy and pastoral care through ministry.
* Opportunity for self progression with high standards for personal behaviours and way of life.
* High standards of qualification for associates who can qualify for membership through mediumship, healing or

by broadly accepting our understanding. Our belief is not just a religion, it is a way of life.

- Readily available healing for all people regardless of their denomination or ability to pay.
- Ordination of ministers. Clerical attire is optional.

Principles:
- Belief in the continuation of life after physical death and in communion with the spirits of the departed.
- Acceptance that individuals are personally responsible for their own actions and spiritual progression.
- Belief in and reverence for an almighty being regarded as creating or governing the universe.
- Belief that spirit energy can be used for healing purposes.
- Pastoral care through ministry to match the individual's needs even if this is not aligned with the minister's views or opinions.
- Confidentiality of information between associates and their clients.

Non-affiliated churches/centres

Generally the people who attend independent Spiritualist churches/centres are diverse in their philosophy of life, although it is based around communication with the Spirit World. Many believe in God or a universal creator, others in Jesus, some even favour Eastern mysticism or meditation, but ultimately they all seek words of comfort, encouragement and guidance from those in the Spirit World.

Philosophy is spoken by the Medium who normally draws upon personal experience or inspirational guidance from their Spirit Guides. The words spoken reflect both the ups and downs of life and how these difficulties can be overcome, often with the guidance of Spirit. Words of encouragement are given to help people cope with life's trials and tribulations, as well as the relating of amusing stories. Spirit philosophy is one of reality, upliftment, finding strength within and not allowing materialism to rule your life.

THE AUTHORS' SPIRIT GUIDES

We thought we would take the opportunity to include some philosophy from our own Spirit Guides.

The following was given in meditation:

> "When I walked upon your world, your Earth Plane, life was much simpler. We did not have the material trappings that you have today, yet we wanted for little. There was love, love for each other that did not hide any greater need or desire. If we were bad or had bad intentions our words and actions were blatant, you knew exactly where you stood. If people were being sycophantic you would know it, if someone did not like you it was not hidden, there was no doubt. Today you can harbour deceit and lies in ways that we could not have imagined. You have pretence, underhandedness and devious methods to undermine those that displease you in any way.
>
> In my time your wealth was measured in your ability to feed your family, in grain and livestock. Gold was merely a decorative element, for Kings and their like. A leader was judged by how well he could sustain his people; food to eat, water to drink. Do you not have the saying 'an army marches on its stomach'? So it was in my day. A well fed army was well supportive of its leader in times of conflict for

they would have no guarantee of things remaining the same under a different ruler. Also there was that element of entertainment; keeping the people amused, happy, content in all ways.

In battle we would see, we would smell our enemy. When you killed a man you would be face to face. Today you can be miles away and kill at the touch of a button. It is almost as if you think that because you do not see the death of your enemy it is immaterial and you bear no scar upon your conscience. Believe me you are wrong. Nowadays you do things to each other, even in so-called peacetime, that we could not have dreamed of, and yet your historians call us barbaric and primitive.

Always you are in a rush. You have forgotten how to take time for yourself; to relax and be at peace. Technology has raced ahead with no conscience or responsibility. It is just another form of selfishness that Mankind inflicts upon itself. They have lost their respect for everything and cling desperately to an ever-disintegrating set of morals and ethical beliefs. You are polluting and destroying the very world on which you rely for your physical existence and those that can help prevent it, those that you elect to represent you, have become the puppets of the materialistic overlords that are the mega-rich, multi-national businesses.

In your materialistic world you breed the negative elements of physical existence; greed, desire, lust for power and control. Rifts open between those that have and those that have not, creating jealousy, envy, hatred and eventually revolt. You even mistake the most simple element: Love, for lust and have lost sight of its purity and beauty.

Mankind is in a state of confusion. It lacks direction and a sense of purpose."

On the subject of meditation, the same Guide gave a brief analogy of why some people struggle to receive images during their meditation:

"In meditation, images are like visitors. They will come in their own time."

Short and to the point as always. What was said ties in with what other communicators have relayed to us in relation to meditation; you cannot force the images through and in fact the more effort you put in, the less likely a result. Be relaxed, be natural, the images will come when the time is right for you to receive them.

And later, on the subject of Spirit beginnings:

"In the beginning of time there was Spirit. To us we were like gods; we had the power and spiritual ability to do and achieve anything. Spirit are naturally omnipotent, for we are non-corporeal, we exist as a part of the laws of existence. Primitive Spirit were raw and lacked the wisdom. Purely by accident a handful of Spirit discovered they could manipulate primitive 'ape' man. It was upon this discovery that all was made clear and our pathway to spiritual progression had begun.

By attaching our lifeforce to the physical body we began to learn hard lessons that moulded our personality, our wisdom enhanced, and through experiencing physical life we began to consider questions that were never asked before in the Spirit World. Those that did not incarnate because of their spiritual advancement ignored the progressive spiritual state of those that elected to experience physical life. Thus the Spirit World was divided between those that were pro-incarnation, anti-incarnation, and those spiritually advanced who just expressed apathy.

So as the Spirit World developed in disharmony those that incarnated and experienced life returned to the Spirit World and elected to help those that remained incarnated. You must remember that Spiritual guidance was given on the current knowledge of the departed Spirit, because no guidance from those considered higher was given. For easy reference we will call them 'Elders'. It was not until the 'era of spiritual enlightenment' that Buddha, Jesus and Mohammed were given the knowledge of Spiritual wisdom, and particularly with Jesus, we tried to explain the existence of the Spirit World in terms the people could understand.

The era of spiritual enlightenment arose as a result of:

1. The number of people upon death that were not returning back to the Spirit World but remaining close to the Physical World in an environment termed the 'Dark Place' (see related chapter).

2. The Elders started to appreciate the benefits of incarnation.

Thus the decision was made to educate people on the Earth Plane of their Spirit heritage and afterlife destiny."

Traditionally the Medium has always been passive with their dealings with Spirit, having the false image that Spirit are perfect and somewhat infallible, but they are not. Our Guides say that the Medium's attitude to the way they develop and their relationship with their Guide should change:

"...by saying to your Spirit Guide, 'Let's try this? Can I do this? Can we do this together?' Spirit have a duty to you. Guides have a duty to their charge; to listen, to help. The Guides would have had to go away, think about it and as a result they in turn would develop. Together you would learn as a team, helping each other. You are a family unit that is growing, developing and learning from each other. At the moment it is not so.

Many Spirit Guides are stagnating themselves because all the emphasis is on <u>them</u>, all the demands are on <u>them</u>, all the time. We make mistakes and sometimes we wonder if we make the right decisions, the right call, because it is so one sided. We become complacent, we stagnate. We do not move in Spirit. We're not like technology on the Earth Plane where things move at a vast pace. In that aspect we are very slow, we are 'plodders'. We are very passive in that way. People are set in their understandings, and their views and it is difficult to change those views. Sometimes risks can be greater because the individual may open themselves up to all sorts of trouble.

So Spirit has to keep things more confined, which is very restrictive for them. By being passive in your relationship with Spirit, you are not helping Spirit. We develop, we evolve at roughly the same pace as you do upon the Earth Plane. We learn and experience things through your eyes and as such we are learning together. If you are passive we learn little for the expectancy is all on us. Hence we stand still, we stagnate and we both fail to gain the potential benefits we have to offer each other as a family, as a team. It is all take, take, take and you should know that sometimes love and desire alone is not enough, because there is a stifling of progression of another and it is not just the fault of the Medium.

And it is time to change that way of looking, to get people to explore their abilities more, to understand them more, because once they start to understand their abilities they begin to understand Spirit more, then their place not only within the society of Spirit, but in the Universe as a whole. Once they start to look more inwards, they will begin to understand themselves more, begin to recognise their flaws and hopefully a more kinder and gentle version of Mankind will develop."

THE EVIDENCE FOR SURVIVAL

"Look on the bright side. It's a good likeness."

THE SCIENTIFIC EVIDENCE

A Scientific Fact

There is a wealth of evidence available to support the proposition that every human being, upon the 'death' of the physical body, continues to exist in the Spirit World. However, it does not suit the powers-that-be within society to endorse the findings that the lifeforce survives in a totally non-organic environment. It is a scientific fact that matter cannot be destroyed it merely changes form under certain conditions. A good analogy of this can be shown using water as the example:

Water can be transformed into steam or ice and then back to its natural state. When water is heated the molecules vibrate at a faster rate, become lighter and transform into steam. The reverse is the case for ice; for when the water molecules are subjected to cold the vibrational rate becomes slower and denser. You, as an individual, are composed of matter that vibrates at a slower rate than that of your lifeforce.

So upon the death of the body the organic material decomposes, it does not disintegrate and cease to exist, but merely returns to its basic form and as such helps to fertilise the soil for the production of new organic material, such as plant life. You are then left with the energy matter of your lifeforce/soul and its release is represented by the change into steam. In this state you are beyond recognition to what is considered the norm with respect to sensory perception (visual, audio, etc.), but as with electricity and air, circumstances dictate when you can and can't see them although you know they are there through their effects upon you or the surrounding environment. Spirit are no different, for in certain conditions you can become aware of their presence.

Public Belief

There is an increase in the number of people seeking Mediums for proof of survival, and in the Psychic News issue, dated December 4th 2004, it was reported that the Daily Mirror newspaper ran a Psychic week and quoted figures in a recent Mori Poll that…;

> 'showed that an astonishing seven out of ten of us are convinced that psychic powers, telepathy and communicating with the dead are all possible'.

At present public opinion does not sway the anti-Spiritualists, for it is not in the interest of religions to openly support Spiritualism in any way. To do so would cause them to lose 'face' in the admission that they had been preaching erroneous interpretations of their religious writings for centuries and that as a result they have been responsible for millions having been murdered in their name.

A Religious Perspective

In his book 'Looking Back' (pg 350), Arthur Findlay recounts a most revealing encounter after he had addressed a large audience in Rome in 1934, chaired by Prince Christopher of Greece:

> "Several high dignitaries of the church were there, one, a cardinal, with whom I had a talk after the meeting, telling me that séances were held at the Vatican, but that the Pope, Pius XI, was a bad sitter, much better results being obtained when he was not present."

The Church of England, in 1937, investigated Mediumship led by Archbishops Lang and Temple. After two years, the Archbishops summed up their findings by reporting;

"The view has been held with some degree of church authority, that psychic phenomena are real but that proceed from evil Spirits. The possibility that Spirits of a low order may seek to influence us in this way cannot be excluded as inherently illogical or absurd, but it would be extremely unlikely if there were not also the possibility of contact with good Spirits."

[Michael Roll's website:
www.survivalafterdeath.org]

And:

"If Spiritualism, with all aberrations set aside and with every care taken to present it humbly and accurately, contains a truth, it is important to see that truth not as a new religion, but only as filling up certain gaps in our knowledge, so that where we already walked by faith, we may now have some measure of sight as well.

We must leave practical guidance to the church itself..."

[www.survivalafterdeath.org]

The conclusion of this investigation was reported by the 'Psychic Press' in 1979 as;

the hypothesis that they (Spirit communications) proceed in some cases from discarnate Spirits is the true one.

This report was leaked to the media in 1979 after being locked away for 40 years in Lambeth Palace because it was considered dangerous by the Church.

Religions are subjective because they are built upon personal faith, understanding and interpretation of religious writings. However, Spiritualism is the only religion that tries to prove, through objective experiments, its own 'religious' claims. Past scientific experiments prove survival after 'death' though with all this mounting evidence it is still very open to debate by modern day sceptics, but we are not, and Spirit are certainly not, frightened of putting our beliefs and claims through rigorous testing.

THE SCIENTISTS

Sir William Crookes (1832-1919)

Crookes was a prominent English scientist. Thallium, the radiometer, and the high vacuum tube used in X-ray techniques, are just a few of the many chemical and physical discoveries he made.

It is interesting to note that after Crookes' death all his research notes were destroyed. Luckily we have the published articles he wrote as well as research undertaken by other scientists around the world based on his findings.

At the time Spiritualism was becoming increasingly popular, the scientists asked Crookes to investigate the Spiritualists' claims. They expected Crookes to announce that Spiritualism was a load of nonsense and fraudulent in nature. However, Crookes was a reputable scientist foremost, and he conducted experiments with Daniel Home who claimed he could levitate and Florence Cook who claimed she could materialise Spirit.

When Crookes first embarked on the investigation of Spiritualism he wrote the article 'Spiritualism Viewed by the Light of Modern science' which was published in the 'Quarterly Journal of Science', in July 1870 and said:

"A man may be a true scientific man, and yet agree with Professor De Morgan when he says: 'I have both seen and heard, in a manner which would make unbelief impossible, things called spiritual which cannot be taken by a rational being to be capable of explanation by imposture, coincidence or mistake. So far I feel the ground firm under me; but when it comes to what is the cause of these phenomena I find I cannot adopt any explanation which has yet been suggested.....

The physical explanations which I have seen are easy, but miserably insufficient. The spiritual hypothesis is sufficient, but ponderously difficult."

In layman's terms; although Crookes was in no doubt about the authenticity of what he was seeing with his own eyes, his scientific mentality struggled to accept it. This was further reinforced a year later when Crookes wrote the following in his article 'Experimental Investigation of a New Force', as taken from the 'Quarterly Journal of Science,' dated July 1st, 1871:

"Among the remarkable phenomena which occur under Mr. Home's (the medium) influence, the most striking as well as the most easily tested with scientific accuracy, are - (1) the alteration in the weight of bodies, and (2) the playing of tunes upon musical instruments (generally an accordion, for convenience of portability) without direct human intervention, under conditions rendering contact or connection with the keys impossible. Not until I had witnessed these facts some half-dozen times and scrutinised them with all the critical acumen I possess did I become convinced of their objective reality..."

Writing in the 'Quarterly Journal of Science', dated October 1st 1871, in his article 'Some Further Experiments on Psychic Force', Crookes states:

> "It is edifying to compare some of the present criticisms with those that were written twelve months ago. When I first stated in this journal that I was about to investigate the phenomena of so-called Spiritualism, the announcement called forth universal expressions of approval. One said that my 'statements deserved respectful consideration'; another expressed 'profound satisfaction that the subject was about to be investigated by a man so thoroughly qualified as, etc...' a third was 'gratified to learn that the matter is now receiving the attention of cool and clear-headed men of recognised position in science'; a fourth asserted that 'no one could doubt Mr. Crooke's ability to conduct the investigation with rigid philosophical impartiality'; and a fifth was good enough to tell its readers that 'if men like Mr. Crookes grapple with the subject, taking nothing for granted until its proved, we shall soon know how much to believe.' "

Crookes continues:

> "These remarks, however, were written hastily. It was taken for granted by the writers that the results of my experiments would be in accordance with their preconceptions. What they really desired was not the truth, but an additional witness in favour of their own foregone conclusion."

Many claims have been made that Home and Cook were fraudulent, but it is difficult today to look at the circumstance and the credibility of those making the claims, and also, more importantly, how honest and honourable a man was Crookes? We know he was a well respected scientist and any defamation of his character only began to surface after he started to support Spiritualism. So we must look at the facts today the best way we can and Victor Zammit, writing in the 'Psychic World' in June 2003, sums it up:

> "The available admissible evidence is that Crookes conducted all experiments with Florence Cook with utmost scientific scrutiny and integrity. His experiments were witnessed by highly credible people. His experiments with Home and Cook were successfully duplicated many years later and in other countries by other skilled investigators and that not withstanding the grave injurious assaults and the plethora of negative propaganda against Crookes, his credibility to-day remains untarnished."

In addition Victor Zammit continues:

> "Further, historical persecution against Sir William Crookes occurred because as one of the greatest scientists ever in history with very high international reputation, enormously high credibility, authority, power and influence, he went public with substantive information that would have destabilised the contemporaneous establishment's orthodoxy in science and religion. Consistent with the historical adage, one extreme created by Crookes elicited an opposite extreme, the powerful retaliation of those who had a great deal to lose - the establishment."

It seems after Crookes' death that allegations were made implying that he had been having an affair with Florence Cook. Naturally Crookes could not defend himself, unless you used a Medium of course, and there was no evidence in the state of his marriage or indeed the relationship his wife had with Florence and her daughters to suggest that Crookes had strayed. Today we would ask, does it matter if an affair had occurred? What is important though, is whether those experiments can be replicated anywhere in the world and obtain the same results? The answer is of course yes, for the experiments were successfully replicated and we will only quote one from Victor Zammit's list:

> "Nobel Laureate Professor Charles Richet, a professor of Physiology at the Sorbonne, confirmed the existence of ectoplasm and inevitably validated Crookes' psychic claims. About materialisation, this Nobel Laureate and expert empiricist definitively stated, 'it's a fact.' "

> [Psychic World, June 2003]

Sir William Crookes did not become a confirmed believer in either Spiritualism or the existence of a Spirit World until he saw Katie King materialise using the ectoplasm of the Medium, Florence Cook.

Florence Cook (1856-1904)

Florence was a Materialisation Medium which means that Spirit uses the ectoplasm of the Medium to reconstruct themselves. Ectoplasm is the etheric energy-matter that the Spirit operators withdraw from the Medium's body and manipulate it. The ectoplasm normally emerges from the Medium via the nose, mouth or the solar plexus located near the navel. This means a loved one that has 'died' can reform themselves to such an extent you can converse with them and even touch them.

Unfortunately for Spiritualism today this is a very rare form of physical mediumship and in the past could take up to 20 years to develop. However, we have been informed by our own Spirit Guides that experience and knowledge gained from the past means that it takes a lot less development time today, although dedication is required on behalf of the Medium and the sitters. This has proved to be a problem nowadays because our lives today are so hectic that we often do not have time for ourselves let alone to sit for physical phenomena.

Florence Cook approached Sir William Crookes to help prove the authenticity of her mediumship. She regularly sat for Crookes until the materialised Spirit form of Katie King moved on and left her Medium. Crookes, under experimental conditions, reported the following in 'The Spiritualist', April 3rd 1874, in an article entitled 'Spirit-Forms':

> "I went cautiously into the room, it being dark, and felt about for Miss Cook. I found her crouching on the floor. Kneeling down, I let air enter the lamp, and by its light I saw the young lady dressed in black velvet, as she had been in the early part of the evening, and to all appearance perfectly senseless; she did not move when I took her hand and held the light quite close to her face, but continued quietly breathing. Raising the lamp, I looked around and saw Katie standing close behind Miss Cook. She was robed in flowing white drapery as we had seen her previously during the séance. Holding one of Miss Cook's hands in mine, and still kneeling, I passed the lamp up and down so as to illuminate Katie's whole figure and satisfy myself thoroughly that I was really looking at the veritable Katie whom I had clasped in my arms a few minutes before, and not at the phantasm of a disordered brain. She did

not speak, but moved her head and smiled in recognition. Three separate times did I carefully examine Miss Cook crouching before me, to be sure that the hand I held was that of a living woman, and three separate times did I turn the lamp to Katie and examine her with steadfast scrutiny until I had no doubt whatsoever of her objective reality. At last Miss Cook moved slightly, and Katie instantly motioned me to go away. I went to another part of the cabinet and then ceased to see Katie, but did not leave the room till Miss Cook woke up, and two of the visitors came in with light."

It must be remembered that the technology in the late 19th century was primitive compared to the technology of today. Sir William Crookes continues with his observations of the differences between Florence Cook and her Spirit communicator Katie King:

"...Katie's height varies: in my house I have seen her six inches taller than Miss Cook. Last night, with bare feet and not 'tip-toeing', she was about four and a half inches taller than Miss Cook. Katie's neck was bare last night; the skin was perfectly smooth both to touch and sight, whilst on Miss Cook's neck is a large blister, which, under similar circumstances, is distinctly visible and rough to the touch. Katie's ears are unpierced, whilst Miss Cook habitually wears ear-rings. Katie's complexion is very fair, while that of Miss Cook is very dark. Katie's fingers are much longer than Miss Cook's, and her face is also larger. In manners and ways of expression there are also many decided differences."

It was reported by Crookes that when Katie told Florence she was leaving and would no longer be using her as a Medium, Florence was extremely upset and emotional. Hardly a response that a charlatan would exhibit.

The reader must remember that anyone can make an allegation of fraud and confessions, but do these allegations test for validity and credibility? Therefore, if Crookes' experiments have been successfully replicated over time, then the reader must doubt the authenticity of the allegations of fraud. However, we cannot rule out the fact that the Mediums of Crookes' era were put under a lot of pressure to perform and a deterioration in their ability to produce the 'goods' could mean a form of income for those Mediums in the late 19th and early 20th centuries was at risk, because often the Medium was not able to find employment elsewhere due to a lack of a proper education.

Today's fraudulent Mediums/Psychics are not driven by the fear of poverty and starvation but by greed, and the promise of a quick buck from those people who are seeking help and knowledge. Such an attitude is abhorrent to those of us who are seeking to gain respectability for our beliefs, as well as to those who work alongside us in the Spirit World. This materialistic attitude is severely damaging the reputations of those genuine hard working Spiritualist Mediums and Psychics.

Materialisation is not to be confused with ghosts/apparitions. This form of mediumship can only be effected through manipulation by Spirit operators. Materialisation is also in the Bible, as is 'transfiguration' which is where the Spirit communicator imposes their face upon that of the Medium.

Matthew 17:2-3

[2] There he was transfigured before them. His face shone like the sun, and his clothes became as white as the light. [3] Just then there appeared before them

Moses and Elijah, talking with Jesus.

Luke 24:15-16
On the road to Emmaus:

[15] As they talked and discussed these things with each other, Jesus himself came up and walked along with them; [16] but they were kept from recognising him.

And later, in Luke 24:30-31

[30] When he was at the table with them, he took bread, gave thanks, broke it and began to give it to them. [31] Then their eyes were opened and they recognised him, and he disappeared from their sight.

John 20:14-16

[14] At this, she turned round and saw Jesus standing there, but she did not realise that it was Jesus.

[15] "Woman," he said, "why are you crying? Who is it you are looking for?" Thinking he was the gardener, she said, "Sir, if you have carried him away, tell me where you have put him, and I will get him."

[16] Jesus said to her, "Mary." She turned towards him and cried out in Aramaic, "Rabboni!" (Teacher).

John 20:26-27

[26] A week later his disciples were in the house again, and Thomas was with them. Though the doors were locked, Jesus came and stood among them and said,

"Peace be with you!" [27] Then he said to Thomas, "Put your finger here; see my hands. Reach out your hand and put it into my side. Stop doubting and believe."

What deciding factors helped Jesus choose the disciples? Spiritualists believe the disciples were chosen because of their mediumistic abilities, particularly the ability to produce physical phenomena.

Daniel Dunglas Home (1833-1886) - Levitation

Home is best known for his ability to levitate himself and objects. The most controversial and famous example of Home's ability occurred in London on December 16th, 1868: Viscount Adare, the Master of Lindsay (later the Earl of Crawford) and Captain Wynne witnessed Home's go into trance, rise out of his chair, float out of one window and float feet first through another window. It was claimed the window was about 80 feet above the ground. Controversy surrounds this incident despite the evidence of the three notable, reliable witnesses, but sceptics have not reliably discredited the account, although discrepancies have been highlighted in the reports of the three witnesses. It should however be noted that even today several people can see the same accident and yet their will be discrepancies in their accounts according to their individual perspective and interpretation of the incident.

Home always preferred to work in light and performed his gifts in front of emperors, peers, poets and scientists. He was accused of being fraudulent and that witnesses to his abilities were somehow hypnotised or experiencing a mass hallucination, yet under experimental conditions conducted by Sir William Crookes, Home was not discredited. Even today amongst the 'non-believers' there is still speculation on how he accomplished these feats. Home could levitate heavy objects as well as himself. Home believed it was Spirit that did all the work to levitate himself and objects and it must be noted that their were times when he openly admitted he could not 'perform'. To give credit to the man he was honest and this does not seem to be the trait of a charlatan who can perform at any time until discovered as a fraud.

Michael Bentine, in his autobiography 'The Reluctant Jester', recounts his experience of seeing levitation:

> "On several occasions there was complete levitation of that weighty piece of furniture. It was raised several inches above the floor, and it *moved* about the room. We had to leave our seats and move with it, for once the light contact of our fingers on its surface was discontinued the table became inert."

Many saints and yogis have reported that during the state of meditational prayer they have risen off the floor. At one time levitation was considered to be the work of the Devil and therefore the unfortunate individual would have been charged with witchcraft. So is levitation possible? Can the brain bring about molecule change, thus either making a person or the molecules around them lighter in order to lift them, as the yogis would have us believe? Or is levitation a result of Spirit intervention and/or molecule change brought about by the power of thought?

Tibetan monks and Indian yogis are often reported to have levitated with such reports readily accepted by the West, yet Mediums producing similar phenomena struggle for recognition. If Home was a fraud, why did other 'fraudulent' Mediums of the time not reproduce this act in the same way?

Frederick William Henry Myers (1843-1901) - Cross-correspondence

Myers was an English psychic investigator and writer. He also coined the phrase 'telepathy' as well as being co-founder and one of the first presidents of the Society for Psychical Research (SPR).

During his investigations, Myers understood the problems Mediums experienced and it has proved difficult to prove 100% the existence of a separate intelligence working through the Medium. So Myers devised cross-correspondence with fellow Cambridge scholars Edmund Gurney and Henry Sidgwick to prove that separate intelligences were operating through Mediums.

Upon Myers' 'death' and return to the Spirit World in 1901, the automatic writings started. In all there were about 12 Mediums selected by Spirit to take part in the experiment. Many of the Mediums were English. They even included Rudyard Kipling's sister who lived in India and the American Medium, Mrs. Leonora Piper. Some of the Mediums never met each other and yet the automatic writings that were produced during a 30 year period seemed to run concurrently when studied together. The majority of the pieces of work were often signed as 'Myers' or 'Gurney'.

When all the separate writings were combined they made sense, and often instructions were given in the writings as well as the claim that the writings were evidence of many complicated designs which were apparently not known to any living person. The scientific conclusion was that it was deliberately designed as a type of written 'jigsaw', with some believing it was from discarnate Spirits namely Myers and co, while others thought it was all by chance.

Since when did a scientific conclusion become chance? The answer is; when it suits the establishment.

20TH CENTURY TECHNOLOGY

Electronic Voice Phenomena (EVP)

This is where Spirit would operate a machine or apparatus in order to communicate. The phenomena was investigated by Thomas Edison in the 1920's, with Marconi conducting similar experiments until his death in 1937. Basically EVP involves the use of a tape recording that when played back allows you to hear the voices of those that have 'died', often responsive, answering questions and using the experimenter's name.

A good example came in 1959 when Friedrich Jurgenson, the Russian-born film producer, was recording wild birds singing, for when the tape recording was played back he heard Norwegian voices discussing the birds singing! The first voices were captured on phonograph records in 1938 and tape recorders in the early 1950's.

Peter Bander, a trained psychologist and Christian theologian, was very hostile towards psychic phenomena until he heard the voice of his mother on a tape recording, then from that moment he was hooked. Bander himself conducted EVP experiments and in 27 minutes some 200 voices were received. Bander believes the investigator acts as the 'Medium' that allows the Spirit communicator to record on the tape.

British EVP researcher, Raymond Cass claims to have contacted over 5,000 voices using a multi-band radio, as well as managing to contact his friend Philip Larkin; a British poet, who convinced Cass that he had not ceased to exist when the physical body had 'died'.

The Catholic Church became interested in EVP in 1952 when two Italian Priests; Ernetti and Gemelli, were recording religious music and heard Gemelli's father's voice on the tape. Somewhat concerned about hearing voices from the so called 'dead', they visited Pope Pius XII in Rome.

The Pope's response is quoted on www.victorzammit.com:

> "Dear Father Gemelli, you really need not worry about this. The existence of this voice is strictly a scientific fact and has nothing to do with Spiritism. The recorder is totally objective. It receives and records only sound waves from wherever they come. This experiment may perhaps become the cornerstone for a building for scientific studies which will strengthen people's faith in a hereafter."
>
> [printed in Italian Journal *Astra*, June 1990, and quoted by Kubris and Macy, 1995:102]

And the article continues:

> "Pope Pius' cousin, the Rev. Professor Dr. Gebhard Frei, co-founder of the Jung Institute, was an internationally known parapsychologist who worked closely with Raudive, a pioneer in the research. He was also the President of the International Society for Catholic Parapsychology. He himself is on record as stating:
>
> All that I have read and heard forces me to believe that the voices come from transcendental, individual entities. Whether it suits me or not, I have no right to doubt the reality of the voices."
>
> [Kubris and Macy, 1995:104]

Another interesting fact Zammit mentions on his website is:

> Since the 1970's the Vatican has continued to sponsor extensive research into all areas of parapsychology including Electronic Voice Phenomena... [and] Father Gino Concetti, one of

the most competent theologians in the Vatican, said in an interview:

'According to the modern catechism, God allows our dead departed persons who live in an ultra-terrestrial dimension, to send messages to guide us in certain moments of our lives. The Church has decided not to forbid any more dialogue with the deceased with the condition that these contacts are carried out with a serious religious and scientific purpose'.

> [printed in the Vatican newspaper Osservatore Romano and cited in Sarah Estep's American Association Electronic Voice Phenomena, Inc Newsletter, Vol 16 No. 2 1997]

What does Father Concetti consider as 'serious religious purpose' when communicating with 'deceased' persons? Spiritualism is certainly a 'serious' religion to be taken 'seriously' as it has been on the Statute Books of England and Wales since 1954 and in 2001 was placed 8th on the list of religions practiced in the UK. As for 'scientific purposes'; Spiritualism must be the most tested religion of all time considering the amount of Mediums that have consented to take part in scientific experiments. Since we meet his criteria, and as a representative of the Vatican Church, is Father Concetti finally giving the seal of approval; that it is acceptable for Spiritualists to communicate with 'deceased persons', as he termed it?

Instrumental Transcommunication (ITC)

ITC is very similar to EVP and is where Spirit try to communicate via computers, fax machines, televisions, telephones; in fact anything that involves using modern day technology. Experiments conducted in laboratories have been extremely successful.

"They are receiving video images on their television sets showing people and places in the spirit worlds... As a result, for the first time in history, we are being shown direct physical evidence of what life is really like after we shed the physical body."

[www.victorzammit.com: Mark Macy - Continuing Life Research, contact Volume 1 #96/01]

An author's personal experience

Back in the late 1980's whilst printing a document, an extra sheet was printed with the word 'Hello' in the left hand margin. In those days word processors were very basic and there was no 'logical' explanation as to how the word could have appeared, as I neither typed the word 'Hello' nor deliberately altered the margin, and there was no-one else at home at the time, that is besides Spirit of course!

In the late 1990's we heard a story about a woman who had just recently lost her mother, and while at home with her young daughter heard the phone ring and her daughter speaking. On investigation she went into her lounge and saw her young daughter speaking on her toy phone. When asked who she was talking to, the young girl replied, 'Nannie'. The woman, if not accepting Spirit communication, could not explain how the toy phone rang, how her young daughter could hold such an intelligent conversation for one her age, and pass on information that only the daughter's mother and grandmother would have known.

Russia

Sheila Ostrander and Lynn Schroeder in their book 'Psychic Discoveries: The Iron Curtain Lifted' informs the reader of the psychic/extrasensory perception (ESP) experiments conducted in Russia over a 70 year period. It seems Stalin was a 'closet' psychic researcher who set the gifted Psychic, Wolf Messing the test of robbing a bank using only his psychic abilities. Messing went into the bank, gave the cashier a piece of paper and mentally 'willed' him to hand over a large sum of money, which he duly did so. Later when the cashier was notified of the government experiment he suffered a non-fatal heart attack!

It was not really until Stalin's death that Russia invested time and money into psychic research and the scientific findings were classified as military. The intention was to see how they could successfully use people's psychic abilities in warfare, in order to control the mind and body.

The cosmonauts conducted successful telepathy experiments in space, the idea being that if radio contact was lost in an emergency they could communicate with each other telepathically. The results of these experiments resulted in a form of psychic development of the mind, known as 'psi' training, being introduced into their normal training program.

Sheila Ostrander and Lynn Schroeder state:

> "...Evolution isn't automatic anymore. It's a matter of conscious choice. Seventy years of Soviet adventures into the far frontiers of psi are beginning to look like part of an evolutionary push, one more nudge to jolt us out of a wholly material view of life. Which is one of those grinning ironies of history. Their massive effort to prove that the wondrous, the strange, even the miraculous are really nuts and bolts material events, came up with extensive proof that they are something else again."

THE MEDIUMISTIC EVIDENCE

Matthew Manning, the renown Healer and Medium wisely said:

"To those who know, no explanation is needed; to
those who do not know, no explanation is possible."
[The Unexplained, by Fraser Stewart]

What is Spirit?
This is as difficult as trying to explain 'God' because the concept
is far beyond our physical comprehension, but here goes: First
of all we need to reiterate the point that upon the 'death' of the
physical body the lifeforce is released and continues its existence
in the Spirit World. We define the 'Mind' as you; the voice in
your head that thinks and makes the decisions that form the basis
of your personality; your lifeforce.

In an attempt to explain this better we use the following
analogy:

You are a very separate individual and substance from your car.
When you get into your car and start it you effectively become
the cars 'mind', and the ignition switches the brain on to await
your instructions. In essence you 'animate' your car. You can
make it do things within its limitations; go fast, turn, stop, etc.,
for together you are working as a team to accomplish a goal; to
arrive at a particular destination. When you reach your destination
you get out of the car, it ceases to be 'animated' and you continue
with your life. Over a period of time the car would eventually
deteriorate if it was never used again, just as the physical body
decomposes.

So in reality, your brain switches on the functions that look
after your physical body. The 'Mind' animates, and gives direction
and purpose to the body to achieve its destination; spiritual
progression. The 'Mind' is the lifeforce (soul) expressing itself

through the body, but it is limited by the functionality of the brain and physical condition of the body. When the body 'dies' all that is left is the 'Mind', so just as when you stepped out of the car, upon 'death' you metaphorically 'step' out of the physical body and continue with your life in a totally different environment. You are now existing solely as pure 'thought' energy matter, without an organic shell to animate, and comprising of your personality, thoughts, knowledge, memories, etc. So Spirit is the lifeforce, which in the Physical World expresses itself through the 'Mind' and in the Spirit World as pure 'thought' energy matter.

How do Spirit communicate with each other?

We established in the previous section that our lifeforce, the 'Mind', comprises of our thoughts and personality; pure 'thought' energy matter. So if we were to see Spirit in their true form it would be as a pulse or rhythmical throbbing. It is almost like a heartbeat and serves to indicate the spiritual progression/evolution of a Spirit being. The faster the pulse/throb, the more evolved the Spirit, seen as a pulsating white or coloured lights. Therefore, our lifeforce has a vibrational rate that is as unique to us as our fingerprints and serves to identify who we are.

The vibrational rate is determined by your spirituality and wisdom as an individual. Just because you live a spiritual life as part of a religious belief system, does not necessarily make you a spiritual person, because you may still have materialistic desires. If you have lead a good and kind life on the Physical World, upon your 'death' your lifeforce is going to attain a faster vibrational rate than someone who has lead a bad or spiteful life. For the more pure in thought and actions you are, the closer you are becoming to the God of spiritual perfection and unconditional love.

When we return to the Spirit World our lifeforce cannot lie, hide the truth or pretend anymore. We are stripped of those physical elements and all we are left with is the essence of our spiritual nature, our true self, and we cannot hide from those aspects we do not like about ourselves. This is all represented in our vibrational rate and as such we are 'an open book'.

Spirit communicate telepathically because they are natural 'thought' energy. As a scenario you have two lifeforces that wish to communicate with each other. One is spiritually advanced and has a fast vibrational rate and the other has a slow vibrational rate because they were selfish and unkind while they lived on the Earth. We will term them Spirit A & B respectively.

Spirit B cannot make their vibrational rate any faster, so Spirit A must slow down theirs to make it compatible with Spirit B's in order to enable telepathic communication to a degree that both will understand. Without making that effort, Spirit A would have effectively been listening to something similar to a TV programme being played in slow motion, the words emanating as a drawl. Spirit B on the other hand, would have received the thoughts as if the TV programme was being fast forwarded, so neither would have made intelligible sense. So the vibrational rates need to be as compatible as possible, so that in effect they are now 'talking the same language'.

Why Spirit make contact with us?

The main priority for contact is to provide proof that those that have 'passed' still exist after the 'death' of the physical body. They do not wish us to grieve for them when it is based on false beliefs. Spirit draw close to bring comfort, encouragement and guidance. Just as those loved ones that are parted on the Earth Plane miss each other's company, so it is for Spirit; missing the company of those they have left behind. What makes it bearable is the realisation that this separation is not permanent, for our destiny is to 'die' having hopefully learnt our lessons and return home to the Spirit World. Remember Spirit like to be recognised, just as the living do and to achieve that goal they use a 'Medium' who is literally on the same wavelength as them, although the term wavelength is somewhat misleading as it is the vibrational rate as determined by spiritual progression.

How does Spirit make contact?

The majority of Spirit communicators will work with their Medium to develop their working relationship. Generally there is a level of spiritual compatibility and not necessarily intellect, between the Spirit communicator and Medium. The more spiritual you are, the faster your vibrational rate of existence is and vice versa. It would be no good if the Medium was of a slow vibrational rate and their Spirit Guide much faster. You would never be able to communicate properly; it would be like speaking two different languages, since both of you would be transmitting on an incompatible vibrational rate.

In our everyday life we misunderstand people, and as a result we sometimes interpret people and situations incorrectly. A good analogy of this is the telephone line; if you have a bad connection you fill in gaps to make sense of the conversation and you may or may not get it right. So why should it not be any different between us and the Spirit World? After all, as an individual your lifeforce is transmitting at a particular vibration, Spirit then try and match their own vibrational rate to your transmission signal. Thus the symbolic telephone line connection is made. The problem for the Spirit communicator now is that neither of you are speaking the same language. To overcome this, the Spirit communicator uses your psychic senses to impress images (clairvoyance), feelings (clairsentience) and thoughts (clairaudience), to ensure you understand the message being conveyed.

Mediumship is not an exact science

So we have established that Spiritualist Mediums link with Spirit communicators in order to obtain information that proves the continuance of life beyond physical 'death' and disproves that God only creates new souls at the moment of conception. It is the use of such communication that opens Spiritualists up to criticism and the questioning of our credibility. Often anti-Spiritualists claim that Mediums 'fish' for information, 'lead' the recipient to confirm details and we would be dishonest if we were to deny that there are instances when unfortunately this does occur. We should point out that this is not always done with dishonest intentions, but as with all walks of life we too have our charlatans. This said, why is it that Spiritualism is the only religion that is constantly harassed, questioned and tested? Why despite all the positive research and results, does this continue to be the case?

The human race is still evolving, developing and learning, just as Spirit and their Mediums are. We know that during the witch hunts across Europe and the USA, many women were killed in the belief that they were in cahoots with the Devil for 'conversing with familiar Spirits'. The slaying of so many women in a religious frenzy severely affected the natural evolution of the psychic senses, and it is only now when there is more freedom given to talking about psychic abilities and the Spirit World, that we are once again experiencing an upsurge in psychic interest and development. In effect, we are starting from scratch again, but this time society, and in particularly the scientific and religious sectors, need to openly accept and acknowledge that our psychic abilities including communing with the Spirit World, are as much a natural part of being human as are breathing, eating and talking.

Michael Bentine's father carried out his own investigation into Spiritualism and Bentine subsequently makes the following comments on mediumistic abilities:

> "It soon became obvious to us, even me, that genuine mediumship resulting in paranormal phenomena cannot be turned on and off like a tap. Its validity

seems to depend largely on the state of mind of the medium at the time and partly on the circumstances in which the research is undertaken. In the case of my father's investigations, the most effective results were obtained in the friendly atmosphere of our own home, where the medium under test felt comfortable and relaxed.

Sometimes it happened spontaneously, and on other occasions, even when the circumstances appeared to be ideal, nothing whatsoever would happen. This did not necessarily mean that the medium was a fake, for in many cases we had previously had excellent results with the same person."

[The Reluctant Jester]

Mediumship is not an exact science because the results cannot be replicated consistently through experimentation. However, scientists fail to consider the point of how Spirit communicators work with their Mediums and that this working partnership is not subject to our current understanding of physical laws, but they are subjected to 'human evolution laws' and are unlike mathematical formulae, because we are naturally flawed, we are inconsistent.

Mediumistic flaws and responsibility
The following are the current problems that we perceive as seriously affecting the standards of Mediumship:

- The Medium that needs to 'fish' for details is a Psychic Medium and not a Spiritualist Medium, and as such there is no link to a separate free-thinking being. Alternatively, the Spiritualist Medium that 'fishes' for details is not confident in his/her ability and should return back to the

'home circle' for further development with their Guides.
- The Spiritualist Medium has become too materialistic and/ or egotistical. When this happens the quality of information received is affected. This may be a result of 'like-attracting-like', or the negative energy creating a barrier thus making it difficult for Spirit to make a strong link with the Medium.
- The Medium who provides information that the sitter cannot accept. In this instance you may then have the scenario where the Medium has linked with the wrong recipient due to poor clairsentience, provides names that cannot be taken due to poor clairaudience, and offers a description of a Spirit communicator that cannot be taken due to poor clairvoyance. All this may be attributed to the Medium's failure to develop his/her psychic ability sufficiently and as a consequence needs to continue in a development circle to attain a good standard of accuracy.
- Spirit can give details that the sitter may not be able to accept, here the responsibility lies with Spirit, and the only way to overcome this is for the Medium to ensure their Guides make sure the information passed on is accurate.

One of our Spirit Guides gave us the following analogy to explain how Spirit work with Mediums during public demonstrations:

You have 35 people watching a Medium work during a Spiritualist church service. Each of those 35 people may have an average of 10 potential Spirit communicators drawing close, consisting of family, friends, Spirit Guides, etc. So in total there are 350 Spirit communicators wishing to communicate through the Medium. The Medium, being clairsentient (sensing), clairvoyant (seeing) and clairaudient (hearing), then 'opens themselves up'; the psychic telephone link is now receiving.

Now symbolically imagine a train coming into a station, with all the carriages filled with the 350 would-be Spirit communicators eagerly wanting to make contact with those 35 people in the church. The Medium links in with Spirit and using clairsentience is drawn to recipient 'A', but clairaudiently hears the name of Rosie, Betty and Gerald being called out by Spirit for recipient 'B'. At the same time, other Spirit, possibly of a strong personality or who, through desperation, see this as possibly their only chance to communicate with someone in the audience, impress images of themselves upon the Medium, despite the fact they relate to recipient 'C'. With all these various forms of communication taking place at once it is no wonder that the result is total confusion for the Medium.

What then occurs is that the original recipient 'A', cannot accept any of the overriding information and the Medium's link with Spirit becomes weaker, and as such harder to discern the information being received. As the lack of acceptance increases, so the confidence falters, panic sets in within the mind of the Medium and a negative barrier develops, making it harder for Spirit to make a stronger connection with the Medium and recipient. This only serves to highlight the benefit of one to one readings where there can be little or no confusion with regards to the recipient.

In these scenarios the Medium is not entirely to blame, because in effect he/she is working blind. There is a strong faith on the part of the Medium in the belief that Spirit know to whom they want to converse. The problem here is that the Medium's Spirit Guides do not have the situation under control and Spirit 'gate crashers' are allowed through. The Medium needs to develop and improve their working relationship with their Spirit Guides, and to establish a system of working together that provides better control and hence more accurate information. Here the Medium needs to go back to the development circle to improve and preferably gain experience through student demonstrations.

Often we have spoken to our Guides and asked what is the point of Great Aunt Agatha coming through, providing marvellous information on their passing and personality, if the recipient cannot recognise or accept them? Is this not a waste of time on both sides of the veil? Spirit recognise this as a problem that needs to be addressed by the Spirit World, but there are no set rules, making it difficult to set a standard because every Great Aunt Agatha needs to be acknowledged. So Spirit would like the Mediums to take more responsibility for their mediumistic development. The next stage of mediumship evolution is to work as a team with Spirit, to push not only their own development but to inspire and push Spirit to their full potential. The message is for the Medium to be pro-active, not passive, and to make Spirit accountable for their actions. As for Spirit; do not blame them when things go wrong, for it should be remembered that the Medium has freewill and must take responsibility for their own actions.

The Medium's responsibility is to develop their psychic abilities to the stage where they have a good working relationship with Spirit and a method of working is agreed that provides accurate information for the sitter. Spirit's responsibility is to the Medium, protecting them from disruptive Spirit beings and organising the potential Spirit communicators so as to ensure that the right ones are allowed to link with the Medium to provide a successful message.

Successful mediumship is reliant upon the spiritual development of the Medium and their motives. We recognise that a certain standard of mediumistic ability should be attained and recognised nationally, thus aiding the elimination of the charlatan who is 'out to make a quick buck'. At present there are many 'raw' Mediums - not to be confused with Psychics - who use their abilities without fully understanding or appreciating their full potential. Often the developing Medium lacks good spiritual guidance and good circle Mediums to act as mentors; to teach and develop them. This is not derogatory to those circle leaders, for often they lack development direction for their sitters as well as themselves. It is currently difficult to find development circles and often the circle leader fills a gap because they and friends want to develop and serve Spirit, and ultimately God.

A factor we must consider is that as individuals we tend to retain those memories that are useful for the future and discard those that we feel have served their purpose. As we get older memories can become distorted and instances that may be important to us will seem trivial to a relative or friend. So, often the likes of Great Aunt Agatha will remember trivial instances, or relate memories that have become vague during their time in the Spirit World.

THE DIFFERENT FORMS OF MEDIUMSHIP

Here we wish to note that parapsychology is the scientific arm of the study of psychic abilities and it is divided into two fields: **ESP** (extrasensory perception) and **PK** (psycho kinesis).

*   ESP involves information being obtained about the environment without any clues being given by any of the five senses. This area covers clairvoyance, telepathy and precognition, amongst others.
*   PK is the ability for a person to influence their surrounding environment such as moving an object without using any part of their body or any artificial device. It is in effect the manipulation of matter using the power of the mind.

We know that the former U.S.S.R. conducted extensive research into parapsychology and how experimental subjects could be trained to a certain level that involved the power of thought energy (ESP) and manipulation of energy matter (PK).

So here we wish to take the opportunity to clarify for the reader that a Psychic in the context of Spiritualism works differently from a Spiritualist Medium. Unlike the former, the latter involves a telepathic link with a separate intelligence to obtain information, namely Spirit. However, some people may class themselves either as a Psychic or a Medium yet have the ability to do either. We strongly recommend that in order to eliminate any confusion these terms should be used in their correct context when people advertise their services. To prevent any misunderstanding one of the following should be stated; Spiritualist Medium, Spirit Medium or Psychic Medium.

Spiritualist Medium: One who has a working relationship with a Spirit Guide, but believes in the philosophy and/or principles of Spiritualism, and generally has their faith based in God.

Spirit Medium: One who receives information from a Spirit communicator but does not have a working relationship with a Spirit Guide. Also he/she does not follow Spiritualism, the characters in the TV programmes, 'The Afterlife' and 'Medium', being prime examples.

Psychic Medium: One who does not have a link with a Spirit communicator and instead links solely into the energies of people, objects or environments to provide a psychic reading.

PSYCHIC MEDIUMS

Everyone has the natural ability to be a Psychic, so it really depends on the sensitivity, creativity and intuitive ability of the person as to how advanced their ability is. A Psychic can link into the vibrational rate being transmitted by the sitter, so in effect the Psychic has made a conscious link with the sitter's lifeforce and information is passed from sitter to Psychic. The skill is in the interpretation of the sensory information received and its relevance to the sitter. The principle is similar to Psychics 'reading' objects and even environments, where people leave energy 'imprints' that are psychically encoded onto objects or the atmosphere of a room, building, etc. Such an imprint is as unique to an individual as a fingerprint.

Psychic readings do <u>not</u> involve any links with a separate intelligence; Spirit. Psychics are prone to 'cold readings' because they may need some clarification of the information they are receiving, as it is not from an independent source, namely Spirit. Developing your psychic senses is essential to further your development in making contact with Spirit communicators. You can give an excellent psychic reading from any object; a mirror, packet of crisps, even a traffic cone. It all depends on how you interpret the object and what you instinctively know applies to your sitter. People are often amazed at how simple it is to do psychic readings, for all you need to do is trust your instincts and go with the impressions you get; easy.

Psychics make excellent tarot readers because often by interpreting the cards they instinctively know what applies to their sitter. In fact most divination tools yield better results if they are interpreted by a Psychic. A Psychic is restricted to the use of the following abilities;

Psychic Clairvoyance
Psychic images: this does not involve a Spirit communicator. A Psychic can take an object and link in psychically to the vibrations of that object and the psychic modem collects the data and the mind of the Psychic receives the images and through interpretation a reading is given. This generally concentrates on past events in the person's life or is associated with the object with regards to ownership or those that have handled it. Object reading is called Psychometry or known as object association which is a form of ESP.

Psychic Clairsentience
Psychic sensing: this is the ability to instinctively feel what is right or wrong, sensing the energies and imprints of an object. Sensing and feeling what a place is like, or the conditions surrounding an event associated with it. There is no sensing of a

Spirit communicator who is imparting information. An example would be meeting someone for the first time and you have taken a dislike to them for no obvious reason. This is clairsentience working on a subconscious level making you feel uncomfortable in that person's company because your lifeforce energies are not compatible.

Psychic Clairaudience

Psychic hearing: this is the ability to hear thoughts within the mind that does not involve a Spirit communicator. For instance, the thought just comes into your mind the phone is going to ring and it does; the name of someone you have not heard from for a while enters your mind, and then you hear from them. To follow on from the example in psychic clairsentience you met someone for the first time and the thought enters your mind 'I do not trust this person'. Psychic clairaudience is often the inspirational/instinctive thought that proves to be accurate.

Psychic Healing

The ability to link in to the energies and bring about a well-being for the person without being aided by Spirit. If you do not believe in Spirit and use for example crystals, reflexology, reiki, massage, etc., to help relax and heal people, then this can be done successfully solely on a psychic level.

SPIRITUALIST MEDIUMS

In contrast to a Psychic, the Spiritualist Medium has no such restrictions and is limited only by their own physical energy and those in the Spirit World with whom they work. Spiritualists work with Spirit beings who have their own personality and character, very separate from the Medium. As a result, a confident Medium who has developed a good working practice with their Guides should never need to 'cold read' because information is being given to them by a separate intelligence. Naturally a Spiritualist Medium also makes a good Psychic because they would have developed their psychic senses, but the quality of information is far greater from Spirit than from a psychic reading.

Mental Mediumship
This can come in either subjective or objective forms and apply to sight, sound and sense:

Subjective: Perceiving information within the mind, whether with the eyes open or closed.

Objective: Experiencing actual physical reality.

A good example of the difference:
Thinking, as in talking to yourself within your mind, is subjective. Speaking those thoughts and thus making them reality, is objective.

Clairvoyance - Spirit link
Spirit communicators give messages to the Medium through the use of images they wish to be passed on to family and friends. A modern day analogy would be the Spirit communicator representing the telepathic modem; where they send thought images to the Medium's mind that acts as the software to recognise the images. Basically the Spirit communicator impresses visual images via the Medium's vibrational rate transmission into the mind of the Medium. The quality of that imagery is dependent upon how compatible the vibrational rates at which the Medium and the Spirit communicator function. Please note that anyone can be a 'Medium' if they have the ability to see images impressed by Spirit communicators.

Clairsentience - Spirit link

When Spirit draw close to a Clairsentient Medium, the Medium can sense the personality, height, age, gender, even the medical condition with which the Spirit communicator passed. The Medium can obtain a lot of information from clairsentience, but the only problem is that at times there is so much sensory information that the Medium can loose a lot of information that the Spirit communicator wishes to relay in a split second.

For those that do not consider themselves to have mediumistic abilities, you may still sense Spirit around. How many people do you know that have said something like; 'sometimes I feel my mother is standing behind me, watching me, while I'm working in the kitchen'?

Clairaudience - Spirit link

The ability to hear Spirit talking. For the Medium, this ability reduces mistakes of misinterpreting symbolic images and the rush of sensory information. However, the Medium does need to distinguish between a separate Spirit individual and the interference of their own thoughts.

How often have you heard your name being called when there is no-one around, or when others are adamant that no-one has called you, and yet your name was both very clear and distinct? Clairaudience is the best ability to have if you are a circle leader, because you will constantly need to refer to your Guides for guidance on your sitters and how best to help develop their ability.

Trance

On a daily basis we enter a trance state; every time we go to sleep and when we wake up. To a lesser degree, even daydreaming can be considered an altered state of consciousness; a form of trance.

There are different stages of mediumistic trance; inspirational, light (overshadowing) and deep:

- **Inspirational talking:** A good indicator to the start of clairaudience and/or light trance. The novice Medium needs to trust the words given to them by Spirit. Any topic can be inspired by Spirit for use in church services during the address.
- **Light trance (Overshadowing):** Spirit do not take total control of the Medium but there is sufficient control to allow Spirit to speak through the Medium. The Medium is still aware of what is being asked and Spirit are reliant upon the vocabulary limitations of the Medium, as they do not have the same control as with deep trance. There is always the risk that the mind of the Medium may interfere and influence answers given to the questions asked by the circle sitters/audience.
- **Deep trance:** Undoubtedly the best state to attain, for it allows the Spirit communicator to take control of the voice box with the permission of the Medium. This method prevents the mind of the Medium interfering with the communicator, since the Medium is not aware of what is being said or is taking place, and as such is the perfect state in which to produce physical phenomena. During this state, questions can be asked of the Spirit communicator freely without any interference from the Medium and be assured Spirit do enjoy a good debate!

Psychic Art

An overshadowing by the Spirit communicator that influences the Artist Medium to draw their features in a way that will be recognisable to the recipient. This is popular especially among Mediums, as they are often able get drawings of their Spirit Guides. If the Medium is in deep trance Spirit communicators can draw themselves directly.

Spirit Healing

Healers that work with Spirit can be either passive or pro-active. When working passively the Healer merely acts as a channel for the healing energy produced by Spirit. A good example of this is distant healing. The Healer need only to focus on the love link and the desired intention to heal, in the knowledge that Spirit will direct and work with the healing energies.

Our Spirit Guides prefer the pro-active Healer who works with them in allocating the healing energy to the sitter. It is a conscious act of joint service and a knowing that this union can increase the healing potential from both sides of the veil. This method prevents both sides from stagnating as they can develop their abilities together to create a better working relationship that is ultimately beneficial for the sitter. It must be made clear that Spirit Healers cannot guarantee a cure, diagnose, offer alternative remedies, nor suggest or encourage a sitter to give up any prescribed medicines unless they are directed to do so by their doctor.

Whatever the method preferred or used, the Healer, in conjunction with Spirit, attempts to alleviate or at least instigate the physical body to react positively to any health problems. Such problems can include disruption to the pulse/vibration of the lifeforce which in turn can misalign the physical body causing discomfort, pain or illness. That is the reason that Spirit Healers work on all levels; mental, physical and spiritual (mind, body and Spirit).

Edgar Cayce (1877-1945)

A well respected Healer and Medium, he was known as the 'Sleeping Prophet', performing contact healing in a trance state. Based in his own Virginia Beach hospital, in 1926 he founded the Association for Research and Enlightenment. Whilst conducting distant healing, Cayce would diagnose patients from only their names and addresses, often referring them to local doctors by name for continued therapy; doctors that he would never have met.

Harry Edwards (1893-1976)

Considered by many to be one of the world's greatest Healers. Spirit Guides who worked with him included the famous French chemist, Louis Pasteur and the British founder of antiseptic surgery, Lord Lister. Based in his home in Shere, Surrey, that was later to become known as The Harry Edwards Spiritual Healing Sanctuary, Edwards passionately promoted what he termed as 'absent healing' and in his heyday it was not unusual for him to receive up to 2,000 letters a day!

He was also instrumental in the foundation of the National Federation of Spiritual Healers (NFSH). Despite the fact he used trance to develop his healing abilities, under the control of his Guide, Reuben, he never did so when performing contact healing. He nevertheless achieved great success, often demonstrating to large audiences, sometimes up to as many as 5,000 in the case of the Royal Albert Hall.

Matthew Manning (1955-)

Probably one of the most scientifically-tested Healers ever, Manning was said to have nearly abandoned his 'gift' as a result. He has addressed both the Royal Society of Medicine and MPs at the Houses of Parliament about his work. Working as a contact Healer, and with a big advantage in his ability to see auras, he would receive information and identify problem areas as given by his Spirit Guides in the form of colour codes; cancer=black, infection=yellow, pain=red, etc. Manning has helped thousands throughout the world including some cases considered incurable by medical doctors. Despite demonstrating an amazing range of psychic phenomena, he now chooses to concentrate his energies solely into healing.

PHYSICAL MEDIUMSHIP

Very popular from Victorian times right up to the 1950's, during times when people entertained themselves in the evenings. Free from the distractions of the technology of today and often sitting in the dark due to poor lighting conditions, the social climate was more conducive to people regularly sitting in séances (home circles) and hence the production of good physical phenomena.

Materialisation

Spirit create what can only be described as a substance we shall call an 'atomic glue', using the chemical structure within the Medium's body. They are able to manipulate this substance to create what we know as ectoplasm. To avoid hindrance with the chemicals of the skin or elsewhere, the ectoplasm emerges through an orifice and it returns the same way. Although there may be slight variation depending on the power of the Spirit communicator, the best way to describe its appearance on exit from the body is that of a fine chiffon. The whole of the ectoplasm spills to the floor forming a disc and then begins to form a column upwards. As it does so, the Spirit communicator 'sculpts' it by thought into its own image, almost as if creating a 'skin' around which to wrap itself, creating the solidity and warmth of physicality.

Minnie Harrison was a Physical Medium who did not charge for her services, so was under no pressure to 'perform'. This allowed her to relax to such an extent that the phenomena produced was of a very high calibre. Her son Tom wrote a book; 'Visits by our Friends from the Other Side', based on the weekly diaries and notes he kept of the sittings. Minnie produced ectoplasm which her 'deceased' sister, referred to as Aunt Agg (Agatha), used to materialise. He writes on page 12 that Doctor Jones wanted to take Aunt Agg's pulse:

"…Aunt Agg materialised as usual. But before we had any time to say anything to her about Mr Jones' request, she turned directly towards him, held out her arm and said she had come that night with the express purpose of letting him feel her pulse!…… Mr Jones was delighted of course to have such an immediate response and there and then felt her pulse. He confirmed that it was quite normal and then added in his typically dry humorous manner. 'Thank you Mrs. Abbott (which he always called my Aunt) you'll live alright.' Aunt Agg chuckled and assured us that he was absolutely right - she is still very much alive!"

Apportments

Objects that materialise during a circle, but they are not confined to just controlled environments as they can materialise anywhere, be of any size or shape, as long as someone can provide the physical energy for Spirit to manipulate.

Apportments also appeared during Minnie Harrison's mediumship. Her son Tom recounts the incident on his mum's 53rd birthday when Minnie had gone to the pantry to fetch sugar. She closed the door and realised she needed something else and so opened the door again, and in those few seconds:

"There at my feet on the floor of the pantry was a mass of lilac blossom - filling the whole floor space and as high as the first shelf - about three feet high!… made up into a number of bunches… they lasted two to three weeks."

[Visits by our Friends from the Other Side -
Tom Harrison]

Transfiguration

Michael Bentine says this about transfiguration:

> "Transfiguration is an eerie form of mediumship when other people's faces seem to superimpose their features over those of the medium in much the same was as a sculptor models a face out of clay. When the phenomenon is genuine, and not a case of a medium pulling faces in dim light, it is one of the most uncanny things I have ever witnessed."
>
> [The Reluctant Jester]

The simplest way to determine the authenticity of transfiguration is to confer with a second viewer, or if possible several other viewers, to confirm that everyone had seen the exact same image(s). If so, there can be no doubt that the phenomena was physical and not seen clairvoyantly by any individual. The image of the Spirit communicator should be distinct from the features of the Medium and the exact same Spirit communicator should be recognised by at least one person present.

Direct Voice

Spirit produce ectoplasm from the Medium to form a voice box that they then use to speak to the people present. Spirit communicators concentrate their thoughts and it is heard through the ectoplasm voice box.

Leslie Flint is the most well known Direct Voice Medium and probably the most tested. He was often tied to the chair with his mouth sealed with tape and at times a throat microphone was attached to try and detect any throat vibration. Flint's mediumship was never proven to be fraudulent and he would give public demonstrations in a hall holding up to 2,000 people.

One of the early indications that Flint was to be a Direct Voice Medium used to manifest itself at the cinema much to the annoyance of the people in the audience who could also hear the voices, and thinking it was Flint talking would ask him to be quiet!

Psychic Surgery

The title is somewhat of a misnomer because a Psychic would only have the ability to assess the condition through reading the energies of the sitter, whereas surgery requires some form of physical effect. A better term would be 'Spirit Surgery' as there is Spirit influence, in one form or another, in all cases. Also the reference to the Medium as a Psychic Surgeon is incorrect because the only surgeons present are Spirit. There are various known methods of both invasive and non-invasive surgical procedures, conducted in both conscious and trance states.

Those working outside of a trance state do so in one of two ways:

- Firstly the Medium can aid Spirit Doctors by providing a physical counterpart to the work they are doing upon the lifeforce of the sitter. The ailment would have been caused by an imbalance between the two elements on which Spirit and the Medium then work; the Spirit and the Physical. Later after the surgery, when the two elements are combined, the balance will hopefully be restored.
- Secondly, the Medium's own physical energy is used as a tool by Spirit to provide pain free 'surgery' albeit invasive or not.

Some Mediums work in a state of deep trance, which allows Spirit to extend control to the manipulation of the whole body and hence the Medium is unaware of what is taking place.

There have been numerous records of Psychic Surgeons over the years, the majority seemingly coming from Brazil and the Philippines. It is reported that the style of changing the vibrational rate of the body to allow insertion of the hands into a patient was originated in the Philippines through Eleuterio Terte and his student, Tony Agpaoa. Both were associated with the Christian Spiritist Union of the Philippines. Wherever their origin and whatever their background, they all have a certain uniqueness to their style or technique:

Lourival de Freitas
Brazilian, carried out painless, invasive surgery using instruments, but was apparently never in trance. His methods stunned the Spiritual Association of Great Britain (SAGB) during a demonstration in 1966.

Brother Benji Belacano
Based in Manila in the Philippines, he performed invasive surgery in trance, using only his fingers and hands as his instruments.

Alex Orbito (1940-)
Filipino, he performed invasive surgery using instruments but was not in 'full' trance; more a case of overshadowing. While demonstrating in the USA, he was imprisoned for performing Psychic Surgery and as recent as 2005 he was indicted for fraud in Canada.

Joseph Martinez
Filipino, he practiced non-invasive 'Mental' Psychic Surgery. He would merely sit next to the patient without contact and focus his energy on the area surgery was to be performed. Using the energy he generated and controlled, anything up to 13 Hawaiian Medicine Men (Kahunas) would operate on the patient, reportedly with amazing success.

José Arigo (1918-1971)

Brazilian, he performed invasive surgery with instruments, working in trance under the control of Dr. Adolphus Fritz whose abrupt, forthright style was responsible for bringing such surgery international recognition in the 1960's. Arigo worked right up to the time of his death in 1971, despite once being jailed for 16 months for illegally practicing medicine.

Even among those practicing now there is a great deal of diversity in the methods adopted. A fact borne out by the four most recognised Psychic Surgeons of today:

John of God (1942-)

His real name is Joao Teixeira de Faria but he is known simply as Joao de Deus - John of God. Based in the Casa De Dom Inacio healing centre in the remote village of Abadiania, Brazil. He works in trance under the control of up to 34 different Spirit Doctors, the principal being Dom Inacio, after whom he named the centre. He performs both non-invasive; just by the placement of hands on head or limbs, and painless, invasive surgery; using an assortment of tools which have been known to include kitchen knives. Spirit alone provide the sterilisation and anaesthesia, and in 35 years of practice there has been no reported cases of septicaemia or the like.

John's success rate is recorded as being 'nothing short of miraculous', in the treatment of a wide assortment of conditions including paraplegia, confirmed by a 'mountain' of discarded wheelchairs and crutches. During operations, other Spirit Doctors perform 'simultaneous operations' upon people in the crowd that are waiting to be seen. To aid the need for an energy-enhanced environment, 30 or more Mediums sit in a meditational state in one of the adjoining rooms, in an attempt to provide the required energy source.

Although a successful businessman, John devotes 3 days a

week and up to 14 hours a day to the centre, without payment, treating tens of thousands at a time. The centre itself is run on a donations-only basis. Not only do patients come from all over Brazil itself, there are also organised groups that travel from all over the world including the UK.

Ray Brown (1946-)

Working under the control of Paul, later said to be St. Paul, Brown has been known to spend anything up to 16 hours a day in trance. He works in conjunction with a team of Spirit Doctors and nurses to provide non-invasive surgery. Paul is able to see within the body to ascertain what is required in terms of treatment and often patients have reported the experience of feeling his hands working inside the body although his physical hands are in view at all times. Some patients have even been known to have temporary scars on the areas of the body in which the surgery took place. With clinics both in England and abroad, he has developed a reputation for the successful treatment of a variety of ailments. One of Brown's biggest advocates was the famous actor Sir John Mills, who was himself cured of a crippling back problem. Through Paul's influence, Brown is also the originator of a healing method known as 'cross healing'.

George Chapman (1921-)

Worked in trance under the control of Dr. William Lang, through whom he had the ability to diagnose ailments before even meeting the patient, much to their amazement. Working with the aid of physically invisible instruments, his work was subsequently non-invasive and produced successful treatments for everything from brain tumours and cancer, to cataracts and arthritis. Chapman's reputation spread worldwide with his increasing success, and in response to the rising number seeking his services, he opened clinics in Europe and the USA. Despite this, he chose to quietly devote himself to his healing, shunning the limelight. However, one noted recognition of his abilities came in 1975 when he received the Spiritualist of the Year award, presented to him by the renowned Healer, Harry Edwards. Chapman was reportedly still working well into his 70's. Despite the advancing years he is still working, although his son Michael takes the majority of the workload under the control of Lang's own son, Basil.

Stephen Turoff (1947-)

Based at the Danbury Healing Clinic, near Chelmsford, Essex, he works in trance under the control of Dr. Kahn and with the assistance of numerous Spirit Helpers. As such he has the ability to perform surgery with or without 'instruments' which have been known to include kitchen knives, scissors or even letter openers to aid the removal of tumours and diseased tissue. This said, he goes to great pains to point out that any contact healing is carried out without the aid of trance. His success has culminated in the building of the Dr. Khan Healing Centre in Fuengirola, Spain, as well as further trips to Europe and Mexico.

It is also reported that through his connection to the Indian sage and avatar, Sathya Sai Baba, various forms of psychic phenomena occur around him. These include lights appearing above the clinic, streams of light connected to patients during healing when photographed; known as the 'finger of God' effect, and the production of sacred ash (vibhuti). In 1991 he was invited to demonstrate at Stansted Hall, home of the SNU. Unfortunately they were not impressed by his unorthodox methods and as a result their President of the time, George Higginson, spoke out in the Psychic News against the use of instruments. A view, incidentally, subsequently supported by George Chapman's Spirit Guide, Dr. Lang.

Psychic Dentistry

A little known form of Spirit Healing pioneered by the American Evangelist A.C. McKaig. The foremost exponent was W. Fuller, who has supposedly healed over 40,000 patients and of whom it was said, just by the touch of the patient's cheek could cause the materialisation of fillings to fill cavities or instigate the growth of new teeth.

Critics of course, choose to believe that Psychic Surgery is at best purely psycho-somatic or even part of a mass hallucination and at worse, fraudulent or nothing more than a hoax. However, they fail to explain why if that is the case, that millions have sought out such surgery and provided testimony of its efficacy. Also there are literally thousands who privately testify to having seen genuine phenomena, but for an assortment of reasons including religious beliefs, preservation of social status, position or career, or even to avoid public and/or private humiliation, choose not to publicly do so. However you choose to put it, the major contention is not the acceptance of Psychic Surgery, it is the power of peer pressure to deny it.

Photographic images

Have you, or has anyone else you know or heard of, ever taken a photograph and then discovered an image of someone that you knew that has 'died' on the resulting print? Believe it or not this is a common occurrence and Bertha Harris in 'From Séance to Science' writes about her experiences with her father who was a part time photographer;

> "Spirit would appear on the negative film, often causing immense problems, embarrassment and expense when the photos had to be retaken."

Bertha use to help her father in the dark room to develop the negative films, but on the occasion that she was unable to assist him, no Spirit appeared on the film. Bertha then realised that Spirit were using the combination of her physical energy and her father's to superimpose their image upon the negative film.

Automatic writing

This involves the Spirit communicator writing through a 'Medium' who is unaware of what is being written. It has also been noted that at times incredible writing speeds are achieved. The leading exponent was Rosemary Brown and classic composers Liszt, Beethoven, Brahms, Chopin, plus many others, wrote classical pieces through her mediumship. In 1970 an LP of the received works was released. Amazingly, Mrs Pearl Curran of St. Louis, USA won a Pulitzer prize for one of her novels produced through automatic writing.

Ouija board

We do not recommend you use a Ouija board especially for a 'laugh', for all users are very much putting themselves at unnecessary risk. This is due to the energies of the sitters being 'raw' and as such can attract a lot of unwanted attention from earthbound Spirits. Many of these earthbound Spirits are curious and confused with their own current condition/situation and do not wish to cause trouble. However, there are Spirits that do have negative intentions; either looking for their next victim or an outlet for their warped sense of humour.

If you do plan to experiment with a Ouija board please make sure you have an experienced Medium present and be aware of any sitters that have the potential for physical mediumship, for these sitters may attract what is known as 'poltergeist' activity. We suggest you call upon your Spirit Guides to protect you.

Spirit responsibility

A good example of the Spirit communicator misleading the Medium as to their true identity is that of the Delphi Oracle. The people of the time worshipped the god Apollo and expected to hear his words of advice, so this is what the people were given.

Spirit are still responding to the requests of a materialistic world. Spirit communicators may choose not to correct false assumptions and can often use the pretence of being someone historically well known if it serves in getting their message across. They are fully aware of what the Medium can accept, or what is a boost to their ego.

Society today is older and wiser than in the days when Delphi was at its height. The onus of responsibility lies with the Spirit World to move forward and recognise the fact that there are too many conmen in today's society. We neither want it nor expect it from Spirit. What we do expect is total honesty from the Spirit communicator, because how can Spiritualism as a religion be respected if Spirit still treat us like they did our ancestors?

Premonitions
Why do we have premonitions? Is this a way our Spirit Helpers/ Guides communicate with us? What would have been the outcome if Abraham Lincoln had heeded his dream, and not been a fatalist in outlook? He certainly would have survived the night of April 14th 1865. Would Lincoln have served another term, or would destiny have intervened and his death been unavoidable, possibly with a change of circumstances, venue, etc.? Premonitions merely serve to prepare us for forthcoming events, however tragic. They are only meant as a warning; a preventative measure, that may be only temporarily delaying the inevitable.

Mediumship: Genuine or fake?
Today you can fake anything; money, clothing, jewellery, art and even facts, but there is always in existence the genuine article; the real truth. All forms of mediumship can be faked, so how can you the reader distinguish between genuine mediumship and fake? The only answer we can give is to assess the results you receive; how they affect you and how much did it cost you?

Spirit are often limited by the mental and intellectual ability of the Medium. This ceases to be a problem when the Medium is in deep trance, where the Spirit communicator is not influenced by the mind of the Medium. Spirit are telepathic and can impress images and sound upon us, as well as allowing us to sense their thought energy. During any of the forms of communication both sides can experience problems. Physically, these include mental and/or emotional barriers created by illness, anger or grief, and from a Spirit perspective, the differences in the vibrational rates of the Medium, Spirit communicator and sitter. This does not always make a Medium a fake, just one that is having a bad day!

Why seek contact with Spirit?

Spiritualism is often criticised over the standard and content of message given to the recipient. A typical example of this is when a Medium fails to connect directly to the intended recipient and so relies upon generalising as quoted below:

> "...They will diagnose headaches, or a need to see the optician; they are not above fixing a row with their gaze, and declaring 'someone here needs to see the dentist', zooming in without error on the traces of childish guilt they have elicited. These observations come to them courtesy of your dead relatives, and it is impossible not to shudder at the banal concerns of the spirits. 'Your Mum likes your new kitchen units', they will tell some hapless woman, who will shift and bleat on her stacking chair, and often shed a tear."
>
> [www.books.guardian.co.uk - Hilary Mantel's essay from the London Review of Books]

The question is; what do we want from the Spirit World? To know our future? How much are they free to tell us? Could we deal with the knowledge that a parent, spouse or child are going to die in a year or so from cancer? Or if your business was going to fail or your house repossessed?

We adopt selective hearing; hearing only what we want to hear and what is personally beneficial to us. The problem is, that like your past, your future contains both the good and bad aspects of life. It should be remembered that Spirit, including our own loved ones, remain around us in order to guide and help, and not to interfere with our lives.

So what is it that we're really seeking? Can it be;

- Proof of survival beyond the death of the physical body; the 'there must be more to life' syndrome?
- To gain the knowledge that our 'departed' loved ones are well, and free of pain and torment?
- That those same loved ones have not merely dissolved into dust but gone on to another, happier plane of existence?
- The opportunity to receive hope and comfort during our period of grief, and feel the benefit and upliftment gained from hearing familiar names, anecdotes and passed events?

Consider this: When it is time for you to pass to Spirit and you are given the opportunity to speak to your son, daughter, friend, etc., you have left behind on the Earth Plane, what would you say? Remember, you have maybe 10 minutes or so in which to impress upon the Medium everything that you want, that you need to say as proof of your identity and continuing existence. Remember also, that due to the abilities of the Medium and/or surrounding energies, just as with some phone lines, reception can be unclear. A poor message can and often does reflect upon the Medium and even Spiritualism in general, because if the recipient cannot understand, identify with, or merely dismisses the message, they may never attend another service/ demonstration/reading.

So, faced with the dilemma of proof or failure from potentially only one chance, wouldn't you use trivia if it proved a point? Take a statement as simple as; 'you changed your mind three times over the outfit you are now wearing tonight.' Simple, yet potentially effective as proof for the recipient. To every other member of the audience it would be considered banal, but why should it be any more than that if it is meaningless to them? How can they evaluate the hope that one simple message can give? Who are they to judge its value? That is the sole right of the recipient.

The quote devalues what are termed 'banal concerns', but would the writer consider the proof to be of better value if a parent of the recipient had communicated about subjects that would have been out of character to them? You see, when you consider our everyday conversations, how much of them are banal? Work, car, supermarket offers, money troubles and that old national favourite; the weather. Banal yes, but they make up our daily lives and relate directly to us, forming part of our identity.

The quote only reiterates the view of many with regards to Spirit communication, but ask yourself this: How would you want Spirit; your loved ones, to prove their continuing existence? Would you want them to materialise before you and hold a conversation, or would you just be satisfied with a banal message that reflected so many conversations that you would have had with them prior to their passing?

Hilary Mantel continues by suggesting means by which Psychics and Spiritualist Mediums manipulate the audience:

> "...they coax assent from their public by a sort of sweet bullying. It is fair to say that most members of their audience are scared witless; they have paid their money for prophecy and supernatural advice, but if fingered they sit staring like demented cod,

struck speechless, and probably unable to take in what is being said to them, let alone process it and make a sensible reply. It looks like the most naked, risible form of public exploitation: but it is possible, even now, to feel pity for the practitioners of this desperate art. It is a sad thing to see a medium hyperventilating, trembling, running with sweat, gasping out messages from the ancestors to the gormless deracinated teenagers of the Thames Valley, who are too ignorant to know their grandparents' names or where they came from. The dead are all around us, they insist, hovering, taking care, taking an interest; but brokering them to the living is a wretched trade. What is the use of the dead talking, if no one has the skill to listen?"

We do not deny that generally the quality/standard of mediumship has deteriorated. Nor do we defend the need for Mediums to 'fish' for information or be generic in their approach. However, what we do accept is that certain criteria must be met to push Spiritualism forward and to gain public respectability. We have certainly seen Mediums struggle to gain or interpret the message from a Spirit link, but never to be in the sort of physical distress to the extent of hyperventilating as described in the quote; a case of poetic license perhaps?

A personal experience of Hope
To those readers who have lost a loved one or friend and miss their company terribly, we hope the following experience as related by Michael Bentine, gives you hope that death is not real, just an invisible veil between two very different forms of existence; one physical and one of energy, pure thought:

"Many people have asked me if I experienced any

assistance from paranormal sources during this tragic and difficult period of my life. I had warned my son twelve weeks before he and his friend were killed that if he flew with Andy Slade they both would die in a plane crash....In one dreadful flash of subjective clairvoyance on a sunny day at home I had 'seen' the crash. Then, after the crash, I was alone in the garden, desolate with grief, and sensed my son's presence. I saw nothing but my heart leapt with joy. I felt him beside me, his hand touching my shoulder. His voice sounded clearly inside my head, 'I'm terribly sorry, Daddy! It was not Andy's fault ...I sensed his overwhelming shock and grief and tried to comfort him. The bond between us was absolute. For a long moment, Gus and I were together. Then, like a loving whisper, he was gone. A flood of tears washed away my grief, and for the first time in two days I felt at peace."

[The Reluctant Jester]

Incidentally, the plane was not discovered with the bodies of Gus and Andy until nine weeks later, and at the time Michael Bentine did not know if his son was alive or not, until his son spoke to him clairaudiently while he was in the garden.

Are scientists unbiased?

What is the role of the scientist within our society? What is their responsibility to society? Our perception is that a scientist should investigate everything, including what seems to be the impossible. What is the point of investigating something that you already know, or a subject on which you have pre-conceived ideas? Scientists should be unbiased, scientific philosophers, seeking knowledge and wisdom. Just because something leaves a 'bad taste' and goes against the flow of current scientific belief, doesn't necessarily mean it has no value. After all, where would we be if Copernicus and Galileo had not stood up for what they believed in when the price for scientific belief could have been their life. Like religious leaders, scientists have a responsibility to society. If you are biased or want a pre-conceived result, do not investigate it. Open your mind and be prepared to discover new laws of nature besides our current physical laws. A good place to start is 'in our own back yards' by looking at the lifeforce (soul) and then what lies beyond it.

Sir William Crookes said about Spiritualism:

> "The subject is far more difficult and extensive than it appears. Four years ago I intended only to devote a leisure month or two to ascertain whether certain marvellous occurrences I had heard about would stand a test of close scrutiny. Having, however, soon arrived at the same conclusion as, I may say, every impartial enquirer, that there was 'something in it' I could not, as a student of nature's laws, refuse to follow the enquiry wherever the facts might lead."
> ['Notes of an enquiry into the phenomena called Spiritualism during the years 1870-73' published in the Quarterly Journal of Science, dated January 1874]

ETVOSISM

"Ooh, let's have a fancy dress party, you said."

ETVOSISM

As mentioned earlier in the preface, ETVOS is the acronym for Enlightenment: The Voice Of Spirit, a creation of us, the authors, and our Spirit Guides. It was difficult to find a novel and suitable term to separate our opinions from others, so until a better suggestion is proffered we have termed our belief structure within the Spiritualist Movement: ETVOSISM.

The basic tenets of ETVOSISM:
* The pre-existence of the lifeforce before physical conception
* The continual existence of the lifeforce after the 'death' of the physical body
* Two-way communication with Spirit
* All spiritual paths lead to a universal Power Source, and ultimately spiritual perfection and unconditional love
* An afterlife is an automatic right of every individual irrespective of one's beliefs, if any
* Importance is placed upon the individual's philosophy of life (ethics) and not the religion

ETVOSISM Philosophy is based upon:
* Individuals and religions taking personal responsibility for their actions
* Respect for individuals, animals, life, property and people's belief systems
* One God fits all - no religion has the right to a monopoly on God as this creates elitism and spiritual dictatorship
* All religions should operate an open house policy to create spiritual harmony, peace and tolerance between different cultures
* There is no individual God to pass judgement
* There is no physical resurrection

- There is no trinity - Jesus had a beginning because all lifeforces pre-exist before conception
- Spirit, created from part of the universal Power Source, expresses itself through a physical body
- The perception of God as a universal Power Source of creation, spiritual perfection and unconditional love
- The belief that the God that is worshiped today should represent spiritual inspiration and ethical guidance

The diversity within Spiritualism

There is a lot of diversity within Spiritualism and therefore it is difficult to speak on behalf of every Spiritualist. Nevertheless, the basic tenets stating that you do not die following the 'death' of the physical body and in communion with Spirit, is held by everyone. Spiritualism provides a natural forum to discuss everything from the normal issues of life to the eccentric, even the downright crazy. So who are we to say what is right or wrong, as long as it is moral and legal? This freedom of thought helps the Spiritualist to develop and grow spiritually. As a result of this diversity of thought Spiritualism, as a Movement, has been criticised in the past because some people believe it is difficult to discern the message it wishes to send out to the public. This probably has arisen as a result of Spiritualism's philosophy of not being publicised via the mainstream media outlets.

Despite its diversity, Spiritualism does not have all the answers and it would be wrong to suggest we do. We are merely a small piece within a much larger spiritual jigsaw, but we are willing and eager to learn, to keep an open mind, and try and live a spiritual life. We are not afraid to recognise and admit the flaws of our beliefs unlike mainstream religions. In fact Spirit communicators embrace criticism because they enjoy debating.

Unlike mainstream religions, we do not have set doctrines to follow, although Spiritualist organisations do have guiding principles that are open to personal interpretation. So what we decided to do was to set out our own perceptions and philosophy on life, based on the many thoughts and ideas that are often debated and discussed by fellow Spiritualists. So some aspects of the following section will be accepted or rejected by the current Spiritualist Movement. It is all a matter of reasoning, and your own spiritual belief and outlook on life.

God and Spiritualism

As mentioned previously, anti-Spiritualists believe that we speak with demons on behalf of the Devil, but why can't it be said that Spiritualists have chosen to do God's work and that God has granted their wish, using them to spread his message? Just because our beliefs are different does not mean they are wrong or bad, only fundamentally different. The ultimate goal is the same; to be in service to God and to obtain spiritual perfection.

How can you tell if someone is in the service of God?

Can service be recognised by an individual's in-depth knowledge of their religious writings? Maybe through their belief in Christ/ the Holy Spirit/Mohammed? Perhaps by their dedication to helping others no matter how small their actions are; a kind word here, a listening ear there? Or possibly by them putting their lives at risk for the benefit of others, on a daily basis or through a singular courageous act? A person may know their religious writings inside-out and never have their faith questioned, but do they truly live that faith?

Sadly our personal experience has been that there is no flexibility or acceptance of other religious beliefs, but the person who can hold their hand out in genuine and sincere friendship to anyone irrespective of colour, gender, age, nationality and religious beliefs, if any, has the love and innate spiritual wisdom from the 'God Power'. Service to God is expressed through action; actions of love, friendship, sharing, acceptance, etc., and not through the knowledge and ability to quote religious text. To truly live a life of devotion and service to their 'God', they need to express themselves through action, for the worst form of action is inaction.

The true religion

Has God ever confirmed that any of the Christian faiths is the true religion? Has God confirmed this to be true of Islam, Sikhism, Hinduism? More to the point; is Spiritualism the true religion? No. And why is that? Because we need spiritual diversity in our lives; to learn from each and every 'religious' perspective. We need the freedom to go into any religious establishment, to enjoy the philosophy and the teachings, to integrate and debate with others of a different spiritual outlook on life. This way, as individuals, we can grow spiritually, moving ever-forward to spiritual perfection and unconditional love. Why is it so hard to have spiritual harmony between faiths? Why do we crave power and control over others?

By allowing free movement and spiritual integration we can begin to understand our religious 'neighbours', thus eradicating unfounded fears of different cultures and their faiths. Surely spiritual harmony must equal spiritual peace amongst nations. Spiritual leaders should be promoting spiritual peace and religious harmony worldwide, but as long as they maintain the elitist stance that they are the one true religion, we will never see world peace. That is, unless the people instigate a change in the way the spiritual leaders of the world not only teach, but also relate to people of different cultures and faiths.

We would say to the religious establishments, open your hearts, update your outlook and perception of others. Do not allow your Holy Books to be used to condemn others. Allow Mankind to not only live in 'physical' peace but spiritual peace too. It is the responsibility of all religions to care for society's spiritual welfare and not drive it back into the 'Dark Ages'; the era of spiritual intolerance. We are supposedly older and wiser, and it goes against the teachings of an all-loving, caring and compassionate God.

Who or what is God?

We do not believe that God is a supreme Spirit being because God has no individuality. Nor do we believe in a God that is going to sit in judgement and decide who is going to Heaven or Hell, who should be rewarded or punished. That said, those men of the Islamic faith that commit atrocities against infidels and even their own faith, are going to be bitterly disappointed when they discover there are no vestal virgins waiting for them in paradise as their reward from Allah.

Spirit tell us that God does not 'talk' to them, there is no telepathic link. You cannot have a two-way conversation with God, for there is no omnipotent being. God is simply the 'Power Source'; the source of creation, the 'ultimate vibrational rate'; the same rate to which all Spirit strive to attain through obtaining spiritual perfection and unconditional love. Once this level of vibrational rate is attained, there is a natural blending/merging with the 'Godhead'/Power Source serving to enhance and evolve perfection. It is also from this 'ultimate vibrational rate' that the forces of the Universe and Natural Laws are created, as well as new Spirit life.

God's image

A problem lies in society's perception of God; one that can proffer love with the one hand, whilst being cruel with the other. In the Bible, how many times does God select one person or one nation to love, while he strikes down or destroys their 'enemy'? The message is clear: God and religion both represent power; one in the spiritual hereafter and the other on Earth. Is it any wonder that followers of the Holy Bible have been responsible for so many deaths in the name of their God? The religious establishment teaches about a God who is elitist; their religion is the only true religion and non-believers are heretics, infidels, devil worshippers, etc., all of whom need to be saved.

God the symbolic mentor

The God worshipped by modern mainstream religions is not perceived as being the symbolic mentor necessary for living a more spiritual way of life in a modern society. The religions have failed to evolve at the pace of Mankind, for what was right in the teaching of primitive understanding a few centuries ago, cannot be held in the same light today. Mankind's perception of God must evolve before we can spiritually evolve, educating ourselves towards creating a human race based upon caring, sharing, forgiving, compassion, helpfulness, and in giving value to peace, kindness and happiness.

The finite aim is to achieve a perfection equal only to our symbolism of God; the ultimate spiritual being that gives unconditional love. God is the key to awakening the innate spirituality we are all born with. God should be the guiding light to achieving spiritual awareness and perfection from within, and not used as a tool to condemn others for their religious beliefs or to murder and maim in his name. Mankind should take no pride in allowing religious interpretations to dictate how to react to each other, showing a lack of tolerance and compassion, and rather than support and embrace spiritual diversity, to fuel elitism to gain prestige and power.

Satan

Are Christians, conveying an elitist attitude, a selfishness, in claiming the scriptures for themselves and that their interpretation alone is the true one? Furthermore, are their attempts to convert others to their beliefs, without allowing flexibility and individual interpretation of the Bible, any different to the actions of those they themselves perceive as followers of Satan? Are they not merely acting in the same manner as those dictators who frown upon individuality and free thinking when it opposes their beliefs.

Evangelists believe Satan is the ruler of the Physical World who will stop at nothing to try and prevent them from carrying out their spiritual mission in the name of God and through the teachings of Jesus Christ. We perceive the term 'Satan' as one that can be used as an excuse for people who wish to avoid taking responsibility for their actions. We are, and have been for centuries, living in a 'blame culture'. Christian references merely depict 'Satan' as temptation, but seem to forget that every individual has the freewill to accept temptation or not. How easy is it for the gambler, the alcoholic, the hedonist to say, "The temptation was too great, I was a victim of Satan." These people should be honest enough to say, "Yes, the temptation was great, but it was my choice and I enjoyed doing it."

By being honest they have not hidden behind an imaginary figure that has formed part of our religious blame culture. Satan is a throw-back to the times when everything, good and bad could be related to the gods. With all the advancements in technology, how far have we advanced mentally and spiritually from Primitive Man; it would seem, not far. Like our ancestors we blame the gods, the only difference is we have narrowed them down to two; the good and bad aspects of life as represented by God and Satan.

Personal responsibility

One of the facts we love about the Spirit World is that there is no physical resurrection, no God sitting in judgement. When you pass to the Spirit World, you retain the same characteristics/ personality as in your physical life, the major exception being that Spirit know exactly who and what you are. You can no longer put up a façade, you are literally transparent, an 'open book'. So if you have chosen to live your life as a physical, verbal or sexual abuser, thief, rapist, murderer, inciter of hatred, with selfish, cruel, malicious or deceitful intentions, then you cannot hide your true self as you can in the Physical World. The assassin, the terrorist, the mean and ill-spirited can no longer hide, can no longer remain faceless, especially to their victim(s).

This is the good part; Spirit existence is eternal, so those that have done wrong have eternity to face their victims in order to make amends, whether the act(s) in question had a direct or indirect impact. Only after gaining forgiveness from all affected, are they able to 'move on' themselves. So this is a warning to everyone who prefers to do a bad or wicked act against another individual; they may end up spending an eternity facing the unrelenting wrath of their victims. The only salvation is that the spiritual progression of the victims is similarly subject to their granting of forgiveness in conjunction to the request of the wrong-doer. Indeed whether perpetrator or victim, spiritual progression is the right of every individual and this is where you are given the opportunity to put right the wrongs of the past.

The Christian-based religions believe that Jesus was 'the redeemer' who sacrificed himself to alleviate our sins and that all who belief in him/God will be forgiven. This cannot be right for it would remove the key element of responsibility and the onus for that lies solely with the individual. The only one that can forgive is the one that has been wronged; the victim.

The responsibility of society

We are Spirit beings expressing ourselves through a physical body and not vice versa. As human beings we should look at the Physical World, not with physical sight and understanding, but with spiritual insight and understanding. We need to value spirituality far above materialism, for materialism should always be subservient to spirituality and not the other way around. Until Mankind changes its values we will always live in a world where wars destroy nations, the criminal fraternity dictates, greed rules and materialism is rewarded. This is the recipe for a violent world that breeds hatred, is extremely unhappy and concentrates on just trying to survive. It all points to the fact we are living in a world of spiritual deprivation.

Religious purpose

In the midst of this doom and gloom are individuals trying to swim against the tide, to make a better place to live in for themselves and their families. These individuals are the minority, the voice in the darkness. The few that are going against the many are trying to persuade them to turn around, to realise that the direction they have chosen to walk is false and that the wisdom, the key to the answers they seek, is in the other direction.

From a Christian perspective, the prime example is Christ and his followers; swimming against a tide that was futile and resulted in Christ's murder. The majority laughed at them and tried their best to beat them down, but over time the tide has turned, the flow is in the opposite direction and the old minority has become the majority. Christianity is no longer the weak and threatened minority, but has fallen into the very same trap of narrow-mindedness, self-importance and arrogance of which they were the initial victims.

What is the point of religion? Is it meant to be set in stone, inflexible, a spiritual dictatorship that takes away your right to question what you believe? Or should the role of responsibility within society be a guiding spiritual light that allows you to question what you believe, and in fact encourage critical debate of the faith to help 'believers' move forward spiritually; to help them find and understand their spiritual pathway in life?

If the Bible was meant for ordinary people, then why was it originally only produced in Latin? Why is it that only the wealthy or well-educated men of the time could read the Bible? These men not only decided the Bible's contents but also how it was to be interpreted in order to ensure their position in society and to guarantee their continued power and wealth.

Religious slavery

Pope Gregory (540-604) personally had 1,000 slaves. Today religious slavery is still flourishing, although subtly, in the form of doctrines and dogmas. Being a devout follower pleases your 'master' because you therefore follow without question. If you dare to question any part of your faith, or express any desire to leave it, you may face being ostracised not only from the Church but from your family and friends too. In some extreme cases you may find yourself hounded by fundamentalists.

The Church and those closest to you should support your wishes and say, 'we think you are making a big mistake, but you must find your own spiritual pathway in life and because we love you we will always be here for you, to support you in any way we can'. After all, is that not what God would want, what a God that is all-loving, caring and passionate would want? For what is the point of 'God' giving us freewill to choose, only to dictate to us? Where then is our freewill? This God is teaching subordination and this brings us back to slavery and spiritual deprivation.

The Spiritualist 'God' is certainly not a slave master but a supporter of freewill and spiritual free thinking.

Religious simplicity

Christ showed us simplicity. He did not need the religious men to tell him what was right and wrong, who he could heal. Christ did not represent discrimination in any shape or form. It is the Churches that have made things complicated.

Like everything else in life, we have a tendency to make things more complicated than is necessary, and this is also true of our understanding and perception of God. Mainstream religious dogmas and doctrines contain a God that is worshipped in different forms. Similarly a dictator likes to be 'worshipped' and the only difference between the two is the belief; one controls our physical existence and the other our spiritual self.

The dictators have 'cornered the market', so the result is that we are forced to suffer both physically and spiritually.

Freewill

Everything in the Universe originates from the same source and as human beings we have the ability to achieve spiritual perfection and unconditional love as represented by the 'God Power'. We can choose to help someone, or deprive them of their property. We can choose to inflict mental cruelty, be brutal, or be kind. It is our choice how we live our lives and how we respect others or not, as the case may be. Of course, however we choose to live our life we have to accept responsibility for the choices we make and the consequences of our actions as a result. Some people would have you believe that your future is set in stone, but how can this be true if you have the ability to be able to change direction in your life with every decision you make. It is what freewill is all about; freedom of choice at all times. It is, for want of a better phrase, 'a gift from God' and as such no-one can take it from you, ever.

THE NEGATIVE ASPECT OF SPIRITUALISM

There can be no better introduction to this section than this quote from one of our own Guides:

> "We expect other religions to be honest and so it should be for us. We cannot hide aspects that may be detrimental to us."

During the periods between World War I & II, Spiritualism was at its height in quality of Physical and Mental mediumship being produced, especially with regard to the Spiritualist philosophy given by Spirit Guides. This was to give hope to the people who were faced with the prospect of death and the knowledge that life continued after the death of the physical body, an area in which Christianity was failing. After World War II, Spirit still continued giving trance talks with positive images of the Spirit World and what awaits us there, along with messages such as; 'You reap what you sow' and 'personal responsibility'. They continually played down the negative aspect of Spirit. The era needed positive thought; too many lives had been sacrificed and murdered in the name of war, why tarnish hope with too much reality? Since the World Wars however, times have changed and the quality of mediumship has deteriorated. Spiritual philosophy has stagnated and we are concerned that the negative side of Spiritualism is being ignored at society's peril.

We believe that due to a lack of understanding and acceptance from mainstream religions, including Spiritualism, there are numerous people whose lives are being made miserable and unbearable through the attention and manipulation of unwanted Spirit. The main problem is that people do not understand what is happening therefore the problem is not being correctly diagnosed. Generally the first port of call is their doctor's surgery, who may prescribe drugs which often confound the problem, or worse still, incorrectly diagnose them as schizophrenic.

For various reasons there are those involved with Spiritualism itself who do not believe in, or refuse to acknowledge the existence of negative Spirit beings, or indeed a negative side to the Spirit World. We are brought up to believe that everything in the Universe has a natural balance/harmony; yin and yang, black and white, dark and light, positive and negative. So therefore, does it not seem reasonable to accept that where there is good, well-meaning Spirit, so too there is bad, hurtful Spirit?

Maybe there is the belief that if all is not seen to be 'rosy in the garden', then people would be fearful of getting involved. Orthodox religions have fed on the fear factor created by their impression of 'Hell' for 2,000 years and it never harmed their numbers. The reason behind wanting to expose the negative side of Spirit, is not to create fear or disillusionment, but to show an openness, an honesty and the fact that Spiritualism has nothing to hide, no underhand tactics to convert or prey on the vulnerable. We offer you the naked truth and leave it up to your discretion, your reasoning, as to whether you choose to accept it or not.

Tunnel of Light
When the body ceases to function and can no longer sustain life, the lifeforce of that person is released and given an automatic opportunity to pass through the light to the Spirit World. This is commonly seen and recorded as a tunnel by those that have had an 'near death experience'. It is assumed that everyone passes through the same tunnel, a spiritual subway if you will, through to the Spirit World. This however is only partly true, for although we can all take the opportunity to move into the light, and indeed that passage is basically the same for all that choose to do so, the individual must create the 'tunnel' for themselves by their intention/desire to follow their loved ones to the light.

Sometimes a Spirit, either governed by choice or in-grained religious beliefs, chooses not to go through the tunnel of light. There can be a variety of reasons why; fear of the unknown, ignorance, failure to recognise death has occurred, unwillingness to leave loved ones and family, and through religious beliefs; waiting for resurrection and Judgement Day, or that the tunnel is the work of the Devil. If a Spirit has lived a life considered evil, wicked, nasty, cruel, vicious or manipulative, then refusal to pass through the tunnel is borne out of guilt or fear of judgement, retribution and accountability.

No matter what your situation and attitude towards your passing, one thing should be made clear; lying between the Physical World and the Spirit World is an uninviting, separate environment that some choose not to acknowledge and which we feel it is our duty to inform you about: The Dark Place.

The Dark Place

You may dismiss our beliefs as total nonsense and that is your right; to express your freewill to decide. Ultimately the truth will only be made clear when you 'die'. So please remember our words upon 'death' and move towards the light. Whatever you do, do not remain outside the light in the area termed by Spirit, for those of us on the Earth Plane, as 'The Dark Place', due to its slower rate of vibration. Should you do so, you may not like the company you keep, let alone the feeling of suppression and oppression that accompanies the inability to move on. This is the place where you need to exercise your freewill and ignore those Spirits that want to feed off your fear and confusion of the unknown.

Unfortunately the consequence of such a decision is that the Spirit finds itself 'trapped'; a kind of self-imposed imprisonment, within an environment that is symbolised as perpetual darkness/night time. This dark, dense environment feels very oppressive, giving rise to feelings of loneliness and helplessness, so it is fitting that our Spirit Guides choose to term it 'The Dark Place'. Other terms used within the Spiritualist Movement include 'Limbo' and 'No Man's Land', serving to describe a place somewhat separated and uninviting. Like all things within our Universe, there is the need for balance; light and dark, negative and positive, good and evil. So it is with the Spirit World; The Dark Place representing the negative side. Unfortunate as it may seem, the harsh reality is that both good and bad can get 'caught' through their refusal to move through the light, due to reasons mentioned previously, but as with all who exist there, they always have the freewill to enter the light should they so wish.

Here within the dense and stifling environment exists all manner of individuals who have 'died'/'passed' from physical life. They have no contact with those that have successfully passed through to the light of the Spirit World because they will have moved on to a lighter, faster vibrational environment as 'beings of light' and as such cannot exist in the density of The Dark Place for any length of time. Also, as with all aspects of Spirit life, it is without time and space, so those within the environment have no concept of the time spent there and may never be aware of the presence of another.

In Plato's 'Phaedo', Socrates reveals that he was aware of what our Spirit Guides term 'The Dark Place':

> "The well-ordered and wise soul follows the guide and is not without familiarity with its surroundings, but the soul that is passionately attached to the body, as I said before, hovers around it and the visible world for a long time, struggling and suffering much until it is led away by force and with difficulty by its appointed spirit. When the impure soul which has performed some impure deed joins the others after being involved in unjust killings or committed other crimes akin to this or actions of souls of this kind, everybody shuns it and turns away, unwillingly to be its fellow traveller or its guide; such a soul wanders alone completely at a loss until a certain time arrives and it is forcibly led to its proper dwelling place. On the other hand, the soul that has led a pure and moderate life finds fellow-travellers and gods to guide it, and each of them dwells in a place suited to it."
>
> [Classics of Western Philosophy]

This is not representative of the Christian 'Hell' where once you are there you remain for eternity. All Spirit retain the freewill to move on through the light to a better plane of existence.

Negative Spirit Link (NSL)

We have termed an unwanted Spirit, who has made a mental telepathic link with a person; a Negative Spirit Link (NSL). A negative Spirit, is someone who was not a very nice person while alive, and has failed for any of a number of reasons, to pass through the light and as a result has become trapped in The Dark Place. What sets a negative Spirit apart from other poor souls is that they are driven by a compulsion to remain close to the Physical World in order to be able to replicate the experiences of their past, sometimes by attachment to like-minded or weak and vulnerable physical beings. A lot of these Spirits are those that have abused their positions of power or responsibility to satisfy their twisted cravings of sexual lust, dominance or control. They tend to be the psychopaths, sexual deviants and destructive elements of the Physical World, who due to their fear of the consequences of their actions choose to remain in what they believe to be the relative safety of The Dark Place.

Just as those that pass to the light 'feed' on the love of their environment, so these darker elements 'feed' on the negativity of theirs. The negative Spirits enhance their 'feeding' opportunities by searching out a suitable victim with whom they can open a 'telepathic' link, for want of a better expression. As such, the links are primarily communication based only and they use the link to manipulate or impress their desires upon their victim. A negative Spirit will attempt to re-enact the situations, the sensations, etc., of their past through the actions and feelings of their victim, whilst the distress caused will give immense pleasure to the perpetrator.

Once a link is made, the negative Spirit assumes control and benefits whether the victim complies with the desires required or attempts to fight. For instance, if a negative Spirit 'feeds' on control, it is immaterial whether it gets that feeling of power by manipulating the victim to be controlling over others or just by the power and control it inflicts upon the victim in doing so. In the worst case scenario it is possible, over an extended period of time, for the negative Spirit to wear down and mentally overpower the victim to the extent that it is possible to manipulate them to cause harm to themselves or others. It is difficult to determine if the negative Spirit is aware or even cares that they could lose their 'meal ticket', as they will simply move on in search of another.

It should be understood that not all heinous crimes are perpetrated by those under the influence of an NSL. We all make errors of judgement, 'covering a multitude of sins' as they say and we all have freewill to decide on what action, if any, to take in certain situations. In recent times, infamous serial killers have claimed that the voice of God or other irresistible voices have told them to kill solely in an attempt to deflect blame. Even having an NSL does not make such crimes excusable, for there is still freewill and with it personal responsibility. Why could they not have sought help when the 'voices' started?

If religions continue to deny or ignore the existence of a Spirit World, they are removing the incentive for negative Spirits to move on. Likewise the insistence on recognising an NSL as the Devil or a demon is of no help to the victim at all. The burning of their clothes or even in the case of the witches of the 17th C, their bodies, served no purpose at all as the link is purely mental and as such cannot be affected by physical pain. In fact the chances are, in the worst case scenarios, the negative Spirit will find the event stimulating or exciting.

Like attracts like
In your daily life you socialise with like-minded people and so it is with Spirit; an attraction to like-minded Spirit. So if you are an honest, caring person, you will attract Spirit that wish to help you on your journey. On the other hand, if you happen to be a selfish, cruel person, you will attract similar Spirit who will spur you on and in doing so will 'feed' off you. For many

of us life continues regardless and we remain oblivious to the influence of Spirit.

The problem arises when people who are 'good' and are psychically advanced unwittingly attract a negative Spirit. They may be feeling low, going through a traumatic period, or even be children who are bullied at school or in the home. In effect, they are sending out thoughts in the form of a cry for help, in an attempt to get the current distressing situation to stop.

Negative Spirit then use this as an opportunity to influence the person, telling them exactly what they believe they want or need to hear, serving only to compound, if not fuel, the situation. The weaker and more helpless the person, the more influence could be placed upon them by the negative Spirit, to the extent that some could be driven to the brink of what the 'victim' considered to be madness. In the worst case scenario, when the victim is at their lowest ebb, they can be influenced to commit suicide. For the negative Spirit it is all a matter of power and manipulation; feeding off the fear of the victim by manipulating their sensory perception.

What makes a person susceptible?
We have found that there is a common theme to what makes a person susceptible to unwanted attention from Spirit:

- The first criteria is that the person's psychic abilities have developed with or without their awareness, enabling them to see, hear and/or feel Spirit.
- The second criteria is that they are extremely unhappy with their life at present, but they do not know how to resolve the issues. This may be the result of an accumulation of events throughout their life but not necessarily rooted in their childhood. The person has just reached the stage where they are in need of a friend/a confidant, or are just extremely vulnerable. Either way

they want to hear confirmation of, and sympathy for, the situation that is causing them unhappiness and worry.

- The third criteria is that the negative Spirit is drawn to the individual because they can either relate to the thoughts being sent out by the person in distress or an opportunity has arisen for them to manipulate the person for their own needs and pleasure, just as they would have used and abused those on the Earth when they were 'alive'.

- The fourth criteria is that the negative Spirit develops a mental telepathic link with the vulnerable person, often sympathising with them and building a trust. If the negative Spirit has created the link on the basis of similar experiences, they will further fuel the situation by exaggerating or saying more negative things about the people around them and thus creating a paranoia in the individual. The worst-case scenario is that the negative Spirit is able to manipulate the situation to the extent that the individual is persuaded to harm someone else or commit suicide. Often the moral code of the individual intervenes and instead results in self-mutilation.

- The fifth criteria is that an individual who is psychically active; especially clairaudient or clairsentient, but is ignorant to the existence and understanding of how Spirit work, fails to strongly deter the unwanted attention of a negative Spirit. The victims fear for their sanity, which in turn fuels further fear that subsequently makes the unwanted link stronger because the negative Spirit enjoys and relishes the fact that they have caused the distress and can maintain the manipulative control. Here the individual should have some knowledge of what is happening, and know that the solution is to be **mentally strong**, take no notice, tell them to go away in no uncertain terms and make it very clear that they have no mental control over you. We understand that it is extremely hard to be strong, especially when the link has developed before realisation of the situation is made. It is a bit like the root system of a plant; it becomes tougher to remove the longer it is left uncontrolled.

Up until the 19thC, religious exorcisms worked because people had a general belief system that recognised God and the Devil. Today, negative Spirit no longer fear or acknowledge the existence of either, therefore they are not waiting for Judgement Day and so for us it is harder to fight back. Exorcisms are becoming ineffectual because as humans we have become smarter, more cunning and more manipulative; traits that remain with us when we die and become Spirit.

Negative Spirits have tantrums like a 5-year-old in the BBC programme 'Little Angels'. When negative Spirits do not get their own way they effectively throw their 'toys out of the pram', except that you are not dealing with a 5-year-old but a Spirit entity who has lived a physical life manipulating people and therefore an expert at 'flexing muscles'. However, as with the parents in 'Little Angels', it is the negative interaction that fuels and confounds the situation. Once you know how to recognise and deal with the problem the situation becomes controllable, then bearable, and in the case of Spirit they give up and in effect 'leave home'.

With reference to groups; those mostly at risk are children, as they are very much 'open' to being impressed, considering it to be natural or something everyone experiences. In these cases the NSL will take the time to manipulate and mould their victim into having the characteristics that best serves their purpose. Also prominent in the vulnerability list are those that are naturally mediumistic; with an ability to 'link' to Spirit in any, or a combination of ways. These people shine out like beacons to an NSL who are searching for victims and if these 'Mediums' are not able to 'close' themselves or learn ways to 'protect' themselves, they are extremely vulnerable. The negative Spirits will impress false images of themselves as Guides, Helpers and even loved ones upon the 'Mediums' in order to manipulate the situation to their advantage.

With reference to individuals; those at highest risk are those that are of a negative persuasion themselves, for 'like attracts like' and the negative Spirits are guaranteed situations and sensations they can enjoy. There are also those that are weak in character and are, for whatever reason, lacking in mental strength. These are the ones most likely to suffer depression, breakdowns and worse as a consequence of the pressure and torment inflicted upon them by an NSL.

Whatever the set-up, it is possible for an NSL to impress feelings, sensations, etc., upon their victims up to 24 hours a day, 7 days a week. Such effects can range greatly including persuading the victim to talk or act in an uncharacteristic way, and invoking emotions/sensations to the degree that the victim is stimulated as if they were of a physical nature. It is also not unheard of that there can be either more than one link to an individual victim, or a powerful link that attracts the attention of several others or a group of weaker ones that create a negatively oppressive environment around the victim. In both scenarios, when the NSLs instigate a situation from which they gain benefit, this is referred to as a 'feeding frenzy', for they are Spirit parasites.

Schizophrenia and NSLs

First of all we wish to make it perfectly clear that not all cases of schizophrenia are a result of NSLs but are mainly symptomatic of a medical condition. However, we believe there is a high percentage of people who have been misdiagnosed as schizophrenic and as such prescribed the appropriate medication. These people are what concerns us, because it could so easily be treated by an experienced Spiritualist Medium.

The author of the website www.rense.com says that clinical

psychologist Edith Fiore believes that at least 50% of those detained in mental hospitals in the United States, are not insane but victims of Spirit possession.

Here we must clarify that Spirit 'possession' is not possible. Spirit is able to manipulate/influence the mind, which in turns controls the brain and its functions; physical expression. We ask the reader to use reason here, for if Spirit could possess a body, they would be jumping in and out of people's bodies as easily as we eat and drink. Who would take control of our world leaders? What if the likes of Hitler, Idi Amin and Genghis Khan, now they are in Spirit, could possess the bodies of President Bush or Tony Blair? It just does not and cannot happen. Even a very strong physical influence can be rectified once the individual realises what is happening to them and that they are not going insane.

More research should be undertaken with Spiritualist Mediums working alongside psychiatrists to determine the best course of action for the patient. Is the patient suffering from the medical condition schizophrenia or from a NSL? Such issues can be addressed and the appropriate action taken for the benefit of the patient. If this was evaluated as research, eventually the results will determine if there is any validity in our claims that some causes of schizophrenia are a result of a NSL.

NSL encounters

While doing our research, we purchased numerous magazines that printed stories submitted by readers telling of their encounters with NSLs. If we accept that stories of 'creatures' that are evil, odorous, and can literally push people around are genuine and not the creative license of either writer or editor, then we must ask ourselves this; is it possible based on our current knowledge? If so, then logically the non-human 'creature' must have existed at sometime on the Physical World. However, we are assured by our Spirit Guides that this is not possible.

What we believe is in fact happening is the 'psychic investigator', as they generally refer to themselves in the magazines, do not have a working relationship with a Spirit Guide, so they are, in effect, linking themselves to the energies and impressions of the place. Therefore imagine this scenario; a psychic investigator is sent to an old building that is very dark and has distinct atmospheric conditions. The psychic investigator has read the history of the place and knows what to expect, so upon entering such conditions the psychic abilities are automatically heightened.

The Spirit entity is strong as a result of the build up of negative energy, and uses this to impress upon the psychic investigator what they are expecting to see and sense. To all intents and purposes, this Spirit entity is playing to an audience and they are in total control. Thus the Spirit is having a good laugh at the expense of the psychic investigator and accompanying team; a bit reminiscent of the naughty ghosts in the film 'Casper'. Spirit also has the ability to create sensory smells. How often have you heard someone say for instance, 'I know my father is still around because I can smell his tobacco'?

We can scare ourselves due to an over-active imagination and the atmosphere of a place, but mainly as a result of the 'unknown'. In effect we seem to be at the mercy of our 'psychic' ability and limited knowledge of the workings of the Spirit World, and for this ignorance we can thank religious suppression. As more freedom is given to explore psychic phenomena and Spiritualism in general, people are having to learn the hard way. Spirit have the upper hand in respect of the years of experience in the use of telepathy/mind influence, but if Spirit make an unwanted telepathic link we can fight back mentally.

So what about those Spirits that are commonly deemed 'evil' and are reported to push people. Spirit cannot have a direct physical effect upon those upon the Earth Plane, although those with negative intentions, such as those classed as poltergeists, certainly give the impression they do. A good analogy of how such poltergeist activity takes place is the tsunami effect. The entity 'draws' the energy away from the 'victim', just as the tide would recede prior to a tsunami. Depending upon the power generated, not just by the entity but also the 'victim' and anyone else present that can be used to generate energy, the energy is stretched to its limit. Then, just as the water returns for the tsunami, so the energy is released and springs back into place with a terrible jolt for the 'victim'. Again, depending upon the power being generated, the effect can vary greatly; from feeling like a sharp push to literally being thrown across the room. It is true to say that negative energy built up in a location, can have a limited effect upon an individual. It is not of a physical nature as often perceived, but merely as a mental influence upon those present.

Many of these experiences can be reduced if the psychic investigator establishes a working relationship with their Spirit Guides and uses it as a means of aiding their protection. It must be noted that some places and situations may require more than one experienced Medium to help the Spirit entity to 'move on' to the Spirit World.

The Sabbath
The term associated with the day that is allocated for religious worship; Saturday for Judaism and Sunday for Christians, but did you know that the term Sabbath was originally associated with witches?

> "The old term for a meeting of witches, probably originally applied to them through hostile association with the Jews, as 'synagogue' was another common name for a gathering of witches or heretics."
>
> [Encyclopedia of The Unexplained]

Witchcraft
The Chinese and Greco-Roman cultures are full of tales of people who could clairvoyantly 'see' malevolent Spirits and who were in effect mobile 'exorcists'.

> "Chinese folk stories are filled with tales of wandering Taoist monks, figures outside the social hierarchy who have totally given up any idea of 'face', who have the uncanny ability to 'read' a person's fate and to 'see' the activities of malevolent spirits. *Hombahomba* diviners in Zimbabwe can spontaneously tell their client's names, family connections, and problems the first time they see the person. Disciples of a *Tsaddiq*, or saintly master, in Hasidic Judaism frequently tell how their master can 'see' a person's soul at the first meeting and recount the course of their past and future lives. The same thing is related about many Hindu *gurus* and spiritual masters."
> [The Illustrated Encyclopaedia of Divination]

This differed somewhat from the beliefs of the African societies:

> "Unexplained misfortune is a direct result of people's hidden anger, greed, envy, and malice. 'Witchcraft' is the result of those negative feelings, conscious or unconscious."
> [The Illustrated Encyclopaedia of Divination]

Primitive Man's life consisted of ritualistic superstition, and applied to feelings that were instinctively driven, basic, expressive and very raw. Negative beliefs, attitudes and emotions were also naturally expressed through rituals within tribal society. This today is termed witchcraft; the practice of directing one's negative feelings, hatred, fear, etc., towards another person through ritual(s).

In our society today, we can see the equivalent of witchcraft taking many forms. One in particular, that is plaguing our streets today, is the ritual of drinking to excess. Through this medium of alcohol binge drinking, negative feelings are being released and directed at others through violent acts. This becomes more dangerous within groups, because our natural, primal instinct is to be a pack animal and prey on those seen as weak and vulnerable.

Witchcraft recognises and acknowledges the negative aspect of Spirit.

> "A witchcraft divination asks the people found responsible for harm to 'own up to' their own shadows and take responsibility for their feelings [negative]."
>
> [The Illustrated Encyclopaedia of Divination]

In essence the Witch Doctor is the tribal society's psychologist/ counsellor, who is well respected within the community. However, with the advent of Christian beliefs being introduced into Africa by the white colonials it brought death to the exorcist/ witch. Christianity made it more popular and uncontrollable by forcing the practice underground, thus stunting the natural evolutionary progression of the faith. In Western society today, we see the practice of Voodoo, black magic and those that claim to be witch doctors, as well as the charging of extortionate prices to 'heal' people.

Recently it was reported in a tabloid newspaper how a woman was conned out of £20,000 by a 'Witch Doctor' who claimed to be able to cure her sick father. It was a shame that this woman, who was so desperate to find a cure for her father, did not try a Healer at a Spiritualist church/centre. Although a cure could not be guaranteed, it certainly wouldn't have cost her £20,000. Please always remember that no genuine Healer would con a person out of money and the more spiritual a Healer is, the more potent their healing ability can be.

The headline in the Daily Mail newspaper, 4th June 2005, read 'Tragedy of girl aged 8 tortured as a witch' which included the following statements:

> "The girl was returned home despite being repeatedly abused during bizarre witchcraft ceremonies."
> "The son of a relative accused the young girl of witchcraft, claiming "she went out at night killing and cursing people."
> "The horrific case has disturbing similarities to that of Victoria Climbie, who was murdered in February 2000."

Both girls were mistreated because it was thought they were possessed by the Devil. It should be noted that the existence of a devil is very much a Christian belief, and as such we wonder how much responsibility Christianity should take because of their insistence that all Spirit are demons and work for the Devil. Until Christianity accepts that there are good and bad Spirits these cases will continue, and young children will be tortured, often resulting in death and all because of a false belief. If those children had been 'influenced' by a negative Spirit, an experienced Medium would have worked with the child, removed the negative Spirit and shown them how to protect themselves from further negative influence. We are disgusted at the mentality of people driven by ignorance and the refusal to accept that Spiritualism is valid.

Here is another example of so-called Christian love: Some

time ago, while undertaking research on schizophrenia, we came across a website where a woman related how her mother who suffered from schizophrenia was stripped by her fellow Christians, and her clothing and possessions were burnt because they believed she was possessed by the Devil. Words fail us, and it makes us angry at the stupidity and inhumane acts that people do in the name of their God. Not once did they consider the feelings of the mother and the embarrassment she must have felt. The daughter concluded that this so-called cleansing ritual had no affect on her mother's condition. We are not surprised.

On June 22nd, The Sun newspaper reported:

> "…The Voice, the black national newspaper, offers the legitimate services of 'clairvoyants' and 'healers' claiming religious powers and the ability to mend broken romances, cure illness, solve money worries and ward off possession."

The Sun continued:

> "Britain has seen a huge increase in Christian fundamentalist worshippers who believe in driving the Devil out of 'possessed' children when problems befall a family."

What are the Christian leaders such as the Pope and the Archbishop of Canterbury doing to stop this appalling practice? We say recognise Spiritualism and train Spiritualist Mediums to deal with genuine negative Spirits.

Voodoo
Originated in Africa more than 10,000 years ago. The original concept was not dissimilar to Paganism in that its connection

197

between deities and the Earth's natural elements helped shape beliefs and indeed tribal society. Today the Western World condemns Voodoo as a ritualistic black art that has its roots in evil and preys on the minds of the weak. This however is not reflective of voodoo's origins but the absorption of the teachings of the Christian religions brought by the missionaries. Only through their teachings did the people get to know of evil, demons, the Devil and the need for retribution. The July 2005 edition of Spirit and Destiny (pg 30) states:

> "Every religion has its perversions, and with voodoo it's no more disproportionate than that. The spirits are seen as superintendents in every aspect of life, and the voodoo priest helps address your prayer to the right spirit.
> A priest or priestess can act as a channel for the spirits who might be called on if a family member is ill or if luck is needed for a good harvest or business venture."

Voodoo is derived from 'vodun' which means 'spirit' in the Fon language of West Africa. The gods and goddesses; the Ioa, are said to have control over strong emotions, death, war and the natural elements such as fire, water, etc. The 'sustainers of life'; earth and water, are vital in all practices and festivals, and are called up by the devotees to help in every aspect of their daily lives. Each of the Ioa has a corresponding Christian Saint, such was the influence of the early Christian missionaries. It is therefore ironic that the teachings meant to educate the Africans away from paganism, have been so well incorporated as to have become embedded into the same primitive pagan rituals. In fact despite the best efforts of their colonial masters, in 2003 voodoo was made the official religion of Haiti.

Cultures that incorporate the likes of voodoo and witch doctors into their beliefs and societies may have fared better without the influence of Christianity. In the past, if a crop failed it was because this or that god/goddess was not pleased, now blame needs to be apportioned; someone must carry the guilt/the sin. As a result you can be guilty by association. If you walked beside the field in which the crop failed, you may have been influenced or controlled by a demon and caused the failure. It is also conceivable that you could be accused by anyone that you have displeased, or who takes a 'shine' to your property or spouse. You could say that Christianity has helped to perpetrate the modern day witch hunts, maybe not on the scale of those seen in Europe, but damaging enough and certainly ferocious in their mistaken piety. Nowadays it should not be happening, there is no excuse for torturing the victim in order to rid them of demon possession. Such inhumane action is being constantly fuelled by Christianity's refusal to accept that not all Spirit are evil.

Religious responsibility

Often devout people try and help those that have led a bad life, and through their own faith try and convince that individual to change their ways and let God into their lives. This is not a bad thing, but we propose that these religious people are failing because they are not prepared to help the demon that they believe communicates via the Medium. Surely a demon; a bad person, has the right to be given the opportunity to change their ways just like their human counterparts.

Let us assume for one moment that the Spirit communicators are demons and thus are working for the Devil. Is it then not ironic that those anti-Spiritualism faiths are in fact fulfilling their own criteria of working for the Devil, because they are not attempting to approach the demon in love, or offering the hand of friendship in the name of their God? Should they not be trying, as Spiritualists do, to persuade the negative Spirit to mend its ways and in essence change sides? So by continuing to deny the existence of Spirit through fear and ignorance, you are only adding to the Devil's work. It is important here to reiterate the fact that Spiritualists do not believe in the Devil or demons, only bad/negative people who continue their life as bad/negative Spirit in the Dark Place.

Religious respect

The irony is that as Spiritualists we try to prove that there is an afterlife, that bears the term 'heaven', and yet we are still slated. We would have thought religious leaders would be pleased that the existence of an afterlife was an actual fact. Why can the other religions not accept Spiritualism? They can still say that their 'God' is the 'true' God, and their afterlife is the 'true' afterlife, just as they always have. Why are they so scared of Spiritualism? Why is so much energy exerted trying to discredit us?

They do not do this to any other mainstream religions and indeed seem to show them at least some resemblance of respect, even though it is not their chosen religion. In that respect we say to them, "don't be hypocritical". If you slate us as a religion, you should treat us no different from the other religions and therefore you should mete out similar slatings to all. The reason Spiritualism is singled out in such a way is that we do not have the power or the wealth behind us, so we are vulnerable; 'sitting ducks' as it were. We are easy pickings, but we will continue our fight for acceptance and the religious respect we believe we deserve.

Communing with the 'dead'

If talking to the so-called 'dead' is the work of the Devil, why do Christians talk to a 'dead' Jesus for help, strength, guidance, etc., and expect an answer of some form or another? Christians may argue that Jesus is the exception, but the reality is he was born, lived and died as a man and his lifeforce would have had to make the same journey as the one he stated that we would all make one day. If they are able to talk to him, then why can't we? If we were communing with a discarnate lifeforce, Christians would say we were communing with a demon, but if we were to say that the lifeforce was the same one they would have known as Jesus, would they then make an exception for us as they would for themselves? Or would they refuse to believe that Jesus would talk to anyone other than themselves and certainly not the likes of Spiritualists? Another case in point for elitism.

Christianity, Judaism and Islam all recognise the existence of Spirits. Their Holy Books are full of experiences of Spirit communing with the living, yet they forbid any form of contact by anyone but their Holy men. Would mediumship among the 'ordinary' people interfere with their religious monopoly? Would it give access to the kind of truth that would possibly herald their downfall? The truth is; that is the reason they fear Spiritualism. We hold the key, the key to the truth, the truth that through their fear of losing their power, status, influence and most importantly their wealth, they have lost sight of their original purpose; the spiritual welfare of the people.

EPILOGUE

If you look beyond our basic belief of the afterlife and Spirit communication, there is so much diversity in thought amongst us, and even we find some ideas strange and eccentric, but within the debate of these differing views we find inspiration. With such diversity within Spiritualism it allows personal spiritual development to proceed at a pace suitable to each individual. The best thing for us, and one of the primary things we love about Spiritualism, is that we are not elitist; we do not claim to be the one true religion that will lead to God and ultimate salvation. We believe that no matter what you faith is, <u>all</u> paths lead to God. No-one has the monopoly on God. We can openly criticise ourselves and our religion, for we recognise our flaws and that we are not perfect. As in all walks of life, you meet egotistical people and those that charge extortionate rates for their services. We do not hide the fact that in this respect Spiritualism does have/attract its fair share of unscrupulous people and those with inflated egos that give genuine Spiritualists a bad name/image.

Some religious faiths condemn Spiritualists, saying we are speaking with demons and working with or on behalf of the Devil. Two of our basic principles on life are;

- Respect for all life, property, etc.

- Taking responsibility for our actions and not to blame someone else; our social environment, God, etc. Yes, we all make mistakes, it is a natural part of our spiritual growth and a step nearer to God/perfection.

Now, if those two common sense values are the inspirational work of the Devil, then our concept of God and the Devil certainly needs to be re-evaluated. Those religious faiths that condemn Spiritualists as working in cahoots with the Devil should take a long, hard look at themselves, put aside their religious elitism, allow compassion, tolerance and diversity within their thinking, show respect to those of different faiths including Spiritualism, and take responsibility for the fact that religion is often the driving force behind war and violence against the individual. History tells us this, today's events tell us this. So how long can an all-loving God support that? A Spiritualist God certainly does not. What is important is not which religion you subscribe to, if any, but how you are as a person and how you treat others.

What gives anyone the right to claim ownership of God? God is for the people and not just the elite. To exclude and condemn others of different religious belief systems is not what God is about. God is about a self-discovery of the spiritual self, in putting that spirituality to its most beneficial use and not in the incitement of so much hatred and injustice in and between our current religions? Surely one God, by whatever name, fits all. Even an atheist has a moral code governed by their own spirituality; that innate spirituality that is in us all and ironically for the atheist, part of God.

Irrespective of whether you are deeply religious or an atheist, it is the spiritual awareness of who and what you are that is important. God is not an elitist, so whoever you are and whatever your beliefs, when you die you will be given exactly the same opportunities as the next person.

Souls have a pre-existence prior to conception and at the point of 'death' we leave our body to continue our pre-existence as Spirit. We rejoin our Spirit family and friends that we left behind to learn spiritual lessons upon the Earth Plane. So we say to the mainstream religions, 'let us put our past behind us, let us all work together for the benefit of humanity. Give credence to Spiritualism, let us be an alternative, valued religion as today's mainstream religions are, then maybe we can all embrace a spiritually richer world.'

Whatever your religion or philosophy on life may be, we wish you all the very best upon your spiritual journey.

GLOSSARY

Agnostic
Somebody who believes that it is impossible to know whether or not God exists as it is not provable either way.

Antiquity
Ancient history, especially the period of time during which the ancient Greek or Roman civilizations flourished.

Apostate
Somebody who has given up or rejected a religious or political belief or allegiance.

Atheist
Somebody who does not believe in God or gods.

Avatar
The embodiment of a God on Earth, especially an incarnation in human or animal form of the Hindu deity Vishnu, such as Rama and Krishna.

Cabinet
A screened-off area used by a Physical Medium during a séance, which allows Spirit to build up sufficient energy in order to produce forms of physical phenomena.

Catafalque
A raised and decorated platform on which the coffin of a distinguished person lies in state before or during a funeral.

Catechism
A series of questions and answers, especially on the principles of Christianity.

Divination
The methods or practice of attempting to foretell the future or discovering the unknown through omens, oracles, or supernatural powers.

Earthbound

Spirit that have for reasons known to themselves, have chosen not to move through the light and remain close the Physical World. They may or may not be negative in nature.

Ecclesiastical

Belonging to or involving the Christian church or clergy.

Effigies

A carved model or representation of somebody.

Empiricist

Somebody who believes that the application of observation and experiment, rather than theory, can determine the authenticity of something.

Ethereal

Heavenly: An exquisite, light, airy, very delicate or highly refined substance, character or appearance.

ETVOS

An acronym for Enlightenment; The Voice Of Spirit, a fledgling organisation created with the aim of raising the awareness of Spiritualism in the public domain.

Exorcism

The act of using prayer, ritual or ceremony in an attempt to drive out evil Spirits.

Fundamentalism

A religious or political movement based on a literal interpretation of and strict adherence to doctrine, especially advocating a return to traditional principles.

Hilkiah

The High Priest of the Temple of the Lord in Jerusalem, during the reign of Josiah.

Home circle

A group of like-minded individuals that sit in meditation and commune with Spirit, in a controlled environment, in order to develop their Mediumistic abilities.

Infidel
Somebody who has no religious beliefs or is regarded as a non-believer, especially in reference to Christianity or Islam.

Lifeforce
More commonly referred to as the soul or spirit.

Literalism
The strict adherence to the basic or primary meaning of a word or text.

Mohammed (Muhammad)
The Prophet of Islam (c.570-632), born in Mecca, buried in Medina and recorded in the Koran. Meeting opposition to his attempts to convert his fellow Arabs from their local gods to the ancient religion of the Old Testament, he was forced to flee to Medina in 622. This flight (the Hegira) is regarded as the beginning of the Muslim era.

Monotheist
Somebody who believes in a single God, as found in such religions as Judaism, Christianity and Islam.

Non-corporeal
Having no bodily substance. Relating to or involving the mind or spirit and not the physical body.

Omnipotent
An all-powerful being that possesses infinite, universal power and authority.

Orthodox
Following the established or traditional rules of social behaviour, philosophy or faith.

Paganism
Originally derived from 'country dwellers'/'villagers', who were considered difficult to convert to Christianity due to their primitive belief that all elements of nature are represented by a god/goddess and as such can be worshipped individually or collectively.

Phenomena

Experiences or events that when observed can be considered as out of the ordinary, exciting interest and curiosity.

Planchette

A small, usually heart-shaped board supported by two castors and a pencil, which when one or more persons rest their fingers on lightly, writes without conscious direction.

Psyche

The human mind as the centre of thought and behaviour. Also representing the human spirit or soul.

Psychometry

The psychic ability to obtain information about a person or event by touching and 'reading' the energy of an object related to that person or event.

Tarot

A system of fortune-telling using a special pack of 78 cards.

BIBLIOGRAPHY

Andronicos, Manolis., The Greek Museums: Delphi, (Ekdotike Athenon S.A., Athens, Greece, 1979)

Bentine, Michael., The Reluctant Jester (Bantam Press, 1992)

Blackburn, Simon., The Oxford Dictionary of Philosophy (Oxford University Press, 1994)

Bowker, John., The Complete Bible Handbook (Dorling Kindersley, 2004)

Cahn, Stephen M., Classics of Western Philosophy (Hackett Publishing Co, 1999)

Crookes, Sir William., Researches in the Phenomena of Spiritualism (Two Worlds Publishing Company Ltd., 1926)
  - Quarterly Journal of Science (all references taken from the above book)
  - The Spiritualist (reference also taken from the above book)

Findlay, Arthur., Looking Back (Psychic Press, 1988)
  - The Rock of Truth (SNU Publications, 1994)

Harrison, Tom., Visits by our Friends from the Other Side (Saturday Night Press Publications, 1989)

International Bible Society., Holy Bible New International Version (Hodder & Stoughton, 1996)

Karcher, Stephen., The Illustrated Encyclopaedia of Divination (Element Books Limited, 1997)

Kardec, Allan; The Spirits' Book (Brotherhood of Life, Inc, 1994)

Meek, George W. & Harris, Bertha., From Séance to Science (Regency Press, 1973)

Occult and the Supernatural, The (Octopus Books Limited, 1975)

Ortzen, Tony., Lift up your Hearts (Psychic Press Ltd., 1990)

Ostrander, Sheila & Schroeder, Lynn., Psychic Discoveries: The Iron Curtain Lifted (Souvenir Press, 1997)

Bibliography

Paine, Thomas., The Age of Reason (Dover Publications, Inc, 2004)

Reader's Digest., Illustrated Dictionary of Essential Knowledge (The Reader's Digest Association Limited, 1997)

Red Cloud., Red Cloud Speaks (Tudor Press, London, 1992)

Roberts, Ursula., Wisdom of Ramadahn (Regency Press [London & New York] Ltd., 1990)

Stewart, Fraser., The Unexplained (Fraser Stewart Book Wholesale Ltd., 1994)

White Eagle., Prayer in the New Age (The White Eagle Publishing Trust, 1978)

- Spiritual Enfoldment 3 (The White Eagle Publishing Trust, 1990)

WEBSITES

www.books.guardian.co.uk
www.dreamscape.com
www.espministries.com
www.galileo.rice.edu
www.genocide.org
www.ipoet.com
www.members.tripod.com
www.paranormal.about.com
www.prairieghosts.com
www.reluctant-messenger.com
www.rense.com
www.stenudd.com
www.survivalafterdeath.org
www.swedenborg.org.uk
www.tibet.com
www.victorzammit.com
www.williamjames.com

INDEX

- A -

- B -

- C -

- F -

- G -

- H -

Index

Hasidic Judaism 194
Haunting of the Presidents, The 78
Hayden, Mrs. 83
Heaven 39, 48, 51, 52, 63, 76, 78,
    174, 200
Hebrew 64
Hebrew Law 42
Hell 34, 48, 63, 97, 99, 174, 181,
    184
Henry VIII 26, 74
heresy 45, 72, 74
heretic(s) 46, 175, 193
Herodotus 62
High Priestess (of Rome) 58
Hilkiah 33, 208
Hindu(ism) 102, 173, 194
Hitler 97, 191
HMS Barham 86
Hodgson, Richard 83
Holland 74
Holloway Gaol 87
Holmes, Sherlock 83
Holy Book(s) 98, 173, 201
Holy Spirit 44, 104, 172
Hombahomba 194
home circle(s) 83, 140, 152, 208
Home, Daniel Dunglas 117, 118,
    120, 126, 127
House of Lords 87
Human Rights Act 21, 89
human sacrifice 31
Hyde-Lees, Georgie 84
Hydesville, New York 82
hypnotism 85

- I -

idol(s) 33, 38, 39
imprint(s) 65, 144, 145
Inca civilisation 31
incarnation(s) 45, 66, 110

India 128
Indiana Territory 78
infidel(s) 174, 175, 209
Inquisition 74
Inspirational talking 149
Instrumental Transcommunication
    (ITC) 131
International Society for Catholic
    Parapsychology 130
Ioa 198
Isaac 32
Isaiah 29, 34, 35
Islam(ic) 17, 173, 174, 201
Israel 40, 43
Italy 57

- J -

Jehovah's Witnesses 50, 93
Jerusalem 33, 88
Jesse 33
Jesus 28, 32, 42-47, 63, 64, 71, 80,
    93, 95-97, 99, 104-106, 110, 125,
    126, 171, 176, 177, 200, 201
Jew(s) 42-46, 65, 102, 193
J. K. Rowling 32
Joan of Arc 39, 43
John 44-46, 125
John of God 157
Johnson, Patrick L. 76
Jones, Doctor/Mr. 152, 153
Joseph 38
Josiah 33, 34
Judah 33
Judaism 193, 201
Judas 96
Jung Institute 130
judgement 37, 48, 103, 170, 174,
    176, 182, 186
Judgement Day 48, 182, 189
Jurgenson, Freidrich 129

Index

- R -

- S -

- T -

- U -

- V -

- W -